Your time is done now

Your time is done now

Slavery, Resistance and Defeat: the Maroon Trials of Dominica (1813-1814)

PAPILLOTE PRESS
London and Trafalgar, Dominica

First published in Great Britain in 2015

A CIP catalogue record for this book is available from the British Library.

Typeset in Freight Text
Design by Andy Dark
Cover design by Andy Dark
Printed by Printondemand-Worldwide.com, UK

ISBN: 978-0-9571187-7-5

Papillote Press
23 Rozel Road
London SW4 0EY
United Kingdom
and Trafalgar, Dominica
www.papillotepress.co.uk
@papillotepress

“Many were brought to Roseau and butchered in cold blood; and there is a well there, which though of sweet water, and in the centre of the market place, remains unused to this day, from a belief that it is defiled with the blood of these unfortunate people.”

Joseph Sturge and Thomas Harvey
The West Indies in 1837

Executed in the market place, Roseau, 1813 and 1814

Guillaume, Buoy, Jean Pierre, Peter, Victor, Joe, Francoise, Adelaide, Ebo, Zabet, Michel, Quashie, Charlie

Acknowledgements

The documents of the Maroon trials of Dominica (1813-1814) that form the core of this book are produced by kind permission of The National Archives, United Kingdom. I was first alerted to these manuscripts by my friend Catherine Lord - for which many, many thanks, since the idea for the book sprang from that first encounter. Various people read the typescript at various times in its development - I am extremely grateful to Annie Davies, Nigel Fountain, Peter Hulme, and, again to Catherine Lord, for their enthusiasm, acumen and encouragement. Proof-reading - and far more - was by Jeannette Page: thanks to her eagle eye and generosity.

My thanks also go to Roberta Allport for research and Ros Asquith for sleuthing. Others who kindly advised on general or specific points are: Gad Heuman, Barry Higman, Lennox Honychurch, Alick Lazare, Lisa Paravisini-Gebert, Diana Paton; and Bernard Wiltshire for his introduction and for many conversations. Appreciations to Lambert Charles for bringing me wahwah and to Louisette Auguiste for showing me the wahwah vine. To Paul Crask and Celia Sorhaindo for our trip to Jacko Steps and beyond.

Andy Dark, the designer, was, as usual, infinitely patient with textual details and infinitely creative in solving visual and typographical problems and for magically conjuring up the cover.

Many thanks to the National Archives, United Kingdom, and its helpful staff and likewise to the National Archives of Dominica in Roseau; the London Library; and the National Library of Scotland. *Polly Pattullo*

POLLY PATTULLO is the publisher of Papillote Press and a former journalist from the UK. She is the author of *Last Resorts: the Cost of Tourism in the Caribbean* and *Fire from the Mountain: the Tragedy of Montserrat and the Betrayal of its People*. She is the editor, with Celia Sorhaindo, of *Home Again: Stories of Migration and Return* and, with Kathy MacLean and Karen Mears, compiled the educational pack, *A Caribbean History: Hillsborough - a Plantation in Dominica*. Both are published by Papillote Press. She lives in London and Dominica.

BERNARD WILTSHIRE, a native born Dominican, was educated at the universities of York and London in the UK; and at the University of Columbia in New York. He lectured in African, Caribbean and Black American history at the University of the West Indies in Jamaica, the City University of New York and Manhattan Community College, New York. He was a University of the West Indies extra-mural tutor in Dominica and deputy leader of the Inner London Education Authority in the UK. He is a former Attorney General of Dominica.

Notes and Credits

The main body of the text consists of transcriptions of documents held in The National Archives, United Kingdom. The memoirs of William Bremner are taken from a typescript of the original. All attempts to contact the copyright holder of these memoirs have been unsuccessful; copies of the microfilm of the typescript are held at the University of the West Indies, Mona (Jamaica), and the National Library of Scotland.

Punctuation has occasionally been modernised for clarification. Stylistic features, such as upper- or lower-case letters, have been standardised. Omissions are marked by ellipses. Editorial inserts appear in square brackets. Square brackets also indicate uncertainties in transcription: missing words are shown as [missing word/s]; illegible word/s are indicated as [illegible]; and "guessed" words are followed by [?].

Abbreviations
The following abbreviations have been used for text references, credits and endnotes:
TNA: The National Archives, United Kingdom
CO: Colonial Office
WB: Memoirs of William Bremner in Dominica
NAD: National Archives Dominica

Picture Credits

Introduction
p1 woodcut: NAD; Neg Mawon sculpture: Lennox Honychurch; landscape: Catherine Lord. p4 abolitionist medal: © National Maritime Museum, Greenwich, London, Michael Graham-Stewart Slavery Collection. p6 newspaper notices: NAD; Hillsborough "runaways" list: Quarry Bank Mill, Styal. p9 © Victoria and Albert Museum, London. p10 Library of Congress
1813 : Suppression of the Maroons begins
pp16-17 Governor Ainslie: British Museum; Ainslie's proclamation: TNA; Agostino Brunias print: © National Maritime Museum, Greenwich, London, Michael Graham-Stewart Slavery Collection. p23 British Museum. p26 Paul Crask. p30 TNA
1814: Under martial law
pp36-37 Jacko Steps: Celia Sorhaindo; Jacko Steps sign: Polly Pattullo; Court House, Roseau: Polly Pattullo; tear out: TNA. pp44-45 Greg family: kind permission of Alastair Rae; Hillsborough works: Syndics of Cambridge University Library; tear out: TNA. pp76-77 wahwah: Polly Pattullo; wahwah vine: Polly Pattullo. pp98-99 NAD
1814: A governor's defence
pp108-109 Lord Bathurst: National Portrait Gallery; Goulburn: © Palace of Westminster Collection, WOA 1549 www.parliament.uk/art; Ainslie: British Museum; sword: Peter Finer catalogue, 2005
1815: Maroons defeated, Ainslie sacked
p127 House of Commons: © Palace of Westminster Collection, WOA 120; p148 © copyright Richard Croft
After: memory and memorials
pp150-151 Independence Day parade: Polly Pattullo; libation: Celia Sorhaindo

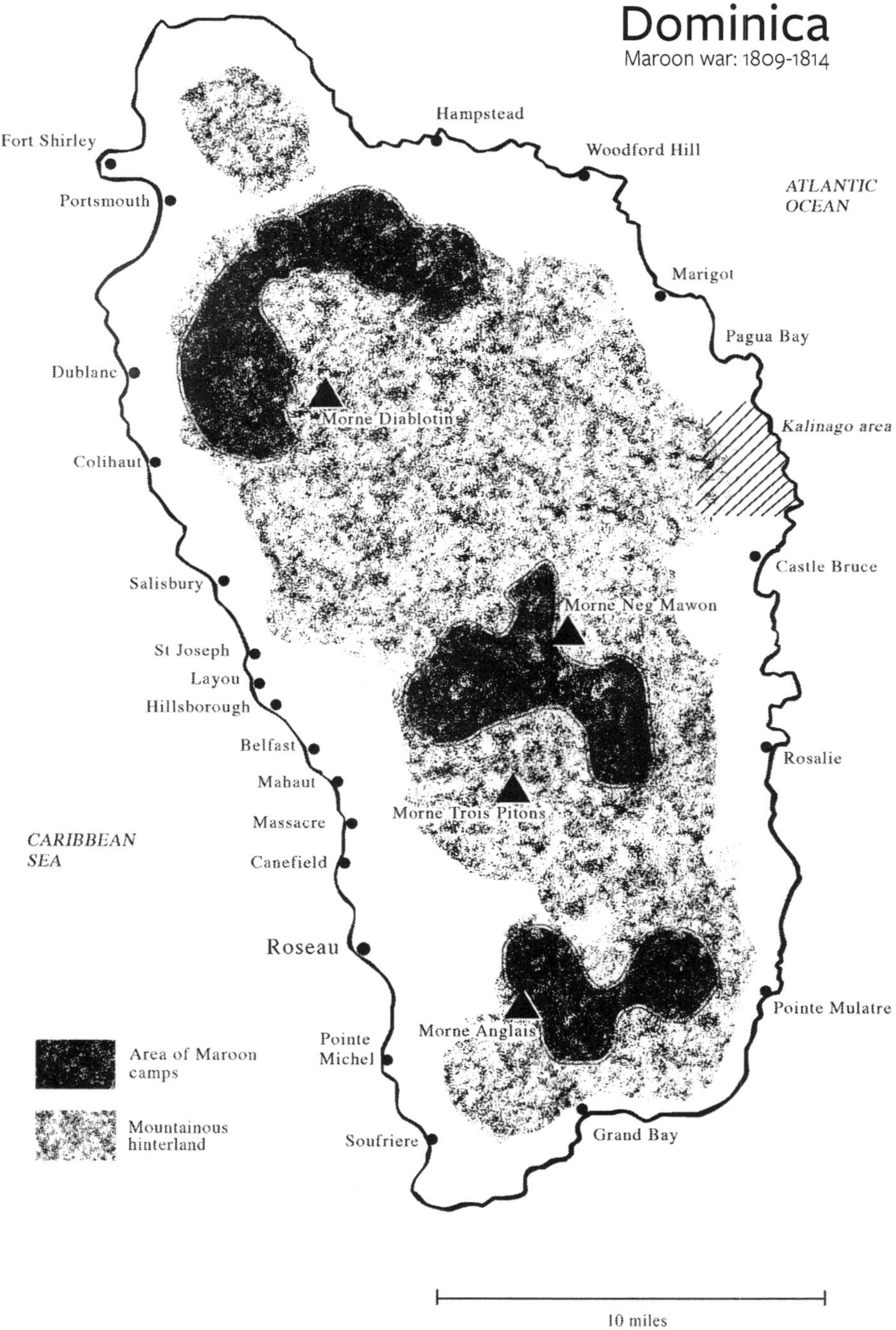
Dominica
Maroon war: 1809-1814
Hampstead
Fort Shirley
Woodford Hill
ATLANTIC OCEAN
Portsmouth
Marigot
Pagua Bay
Dublanc
Morne Diablotin
Kalinago area
Colihaut
Castle Bruce
Salisbury
Morne Neg Mawon
St Joseph
Layou
Hillsborough
Belfast
Rosalie
Mahaut
Morne Trois Pitons
Massacre
CARIBBEAN SEA
Canefield
Roseau
Pointe Mulatre
Morne Anglais
Pointe Michel
Area of Maroon camps
Mountainous hinterland
Grand Bay
Soufriere
10 miles

Contents

Introduction

'Your Time Is Done Now' is a book about resistance to slavery. Not much is known of the men and women who participated in this struggle and made their own Maroon communities on the Caribbean island of Dominica for their voices have remained hidden from history. But through the transcripts of the trials (held in 1813 and 1814) and published here for the first time, we hear the stories of those who had lived as free people in the forests as they stood in the dock.

The trials (both civil and military) were held by the British colonial government in their war against the Maroons, and in this written evidence of the processes (and excesses) of colonial law, we discover why the enslaved ran away, how they lived, survived, and died, and importantly, about the symbiotic relationships between the Maroons and the enslaved on the estates. Most revealingly we hear their voices, even if filtered through the colonial authority.

The title, "Your Time Is Done Now", is taken from the exact words of a slave called Peter at his trial in January 1814. Peter, from Hillsborough estate at the mouth of the Layou River, was charged and convicted of "exciting a mutiny". He was not, in fact, a Maroon but an enslaved fisherman, yet his association with the other slaves (charged with being "runaways") at Hillsborough, and with Maroons, his ability to manipulate the situation and what might be seen as his contempt for the authorities was enough to ensure his capital conviction. We learn more from the evidence of his trial, however incomplete, than we ever can from the slave registers where human beings are listed as chattels.

At the same time, those words "Your Time Is Done Now" could have been spoken by the British governor, Major-General George Ainslie, the Maroons' nemesis, whose adversarial and illegal actions ensured the end of the most direct form of African resistance to slavery in Dominica.

Marronage occurred wherever slavery existed. Those who could, escaped by running away. In many instances enslaved Africans sought a break from the drudgery of plantation hard labour by decamping for hours or days or weeks or months before returning to the plantation: this has been referred to as "petit marronage". The classic Maroon, however, treated his decampment as a permanent thing and was prepared to confront the opposing threat with force of arms. The word, which comes from the Spanish *cimarrón*, was first used in Hispaniola to refer to feral cattle. It was later applied to fugitive indigenous people and then came to refer exclusively to Africans fleeing from plantation slavery.

In the New World, Maroon movements developed as a response of African captives to plantation slavery. Where the terrain was favourable, preferably mountainous and remote and beyond the reach of the slavers, Maroons could build thriving communities as they did in the Cockpit Country of Jamaica, or the hilly borderland between Haiti and what was then Santo Domingo, or in the jungles of Brazil or Surinam and the Guyanas.

The stage in Dominica was not so large but it was ideal Maroon country with its exceptionally mountainous landscape covered in rainforest and cut with rivers. The Maroons were defeated but their years in the forest were not without gain and they left a legacy with which we have yet to come to terms. They were the main challengers, for decades, to the institution of slavery, and, for the right to live in freedom, they were prepared to die.

The Maroons of Dominica were considered the best organised among Caribbean resistance fighters after those of Jamaica, who won their freedom after negotiations with the British. They followed in the footsteps of their predecessors, the indigenous Kalinagos, who had fought to maintain their independence from the white tormentors. In Dominica the Maroons achieved a level of military and social organisation as well as agricultural production which surprised the white planters. They were also able to conduct something akin to a "black economy" among the enslaved population, based on an exchange of goods and information.

Historians have marvelled at the relative speed with which the Maroons

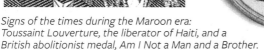

Signs of the times during the Maroon era: Toussaint Louverture, the liberator of Haiti, and a British abolitionist medal, Am I Not a Man and a Brother.

proceeded to develop a "civil society" even within the emergency of being hunted. We see this perhaps in the large number of women and children in the camps and in the extensive cultivations achieved by some Maroon communities - their provision grounds "at one place alone presented to the eye an extent of four miles of the finest plants".[1] The political culture of each camp, however, was military as was necessitated by the situation.

Their chief enemy, Governor Ainslie (1776-1839), who arrived on the island in 1813, was forced to acknowledge their importance, albeit in an attempt to justify the measures he took to eliminate them. Asked by his boss, Lord Bathurst, the Secretary of State for War and the Colonies, to account for his declaration of martial law, he tried to explain his view of the Maroons. "People ignorant of the state of Dominica erroneously believe, that the runaways are slaves, who to avoid punishment for some venial or menial offence, from a harsh master, run to the woods for a short time, and then return to their duty, a few unfortunate, persecuted beings without concert, whose only inheritance is slavery whose condition demands our pity... No misapprehension, Sir, can be greater. They are a banditti under government of a chief, sub-chiefs and captains, inhabiting a country difficult beyond description, having regular outposts or camps as they are called, in advance of the Grand cantonment where the chief resides, with provision grounds cleared for miles. This 'imperium in imperio' has been established above 30 years."[2]

Ainslie's reference to an "imperium in imperio" (a state within a state) introduces an interesting new concept to an understanding of the place of the Maroons in 18th and early 19th-century Dominica. Had he not been under pressure to explain his actions to his superiors in London, we might never have had such a concession. To call the Maroons a "state within a state" undermined the slavers' pretence that the Maroons were mere "banditti", a criminal element who had fallen foul of a legal system to which they owed some sort of allegiance. But the trial transcripts confirm that the Maroons did not recognise the legitimacy of the slavers' law, and they showed this not only in acts of defiance but in the manner in which they displayed that defiance - with contempt.

In the same letter, Ainslie went on to define the real bone of contention between the authority of the British state and the Maroons: the latter's attempt to mobilise the enslaved on the plantations to overthrow the power of the slave state. "It is the practice of these people to increase their number, by enticing from their masters well disposed Negroes... unfortunately they succeed too well, to the great loss of the planters, of whom a few months ago one advertised his estate for sale, in the gazette as 'his slaves had all run to the woods'."[3] Another slaver was even more to the point: "The Maroon Negroes from their frequent communications with the slaves upon the several estates, had caused such a spirit of insubordination that the most serious and alarming consequences were to be apprehended..."[4]

Both sides understood the centrality of this strategy; for on it the success or failure of the parties depended. Thus the Maroons confined their attacks to the softer economic target - the plantations - rather than to the military garrisons. They understood that the support of the mass of the enslaved was necessary to overthrow the system and that without it they would barely survive, if at all. This point emerges clearly in the trials of 1813 and 1814.

If the trials marked the end of marronage in Dominica, its beginnings can be traced to the 16th century when Africans, escaped from neighbouring and already colonised islands, sought sanctuary there. But it was when the British took control in 1763 that marronage expanded and changed in character - they had been free; now they were hunted and regarded as "runaways". Plantation relationships changed too. When the Jesuits sold their slave plantation, "Les Jesuits", in Grand Bay, in the south of the island, to incoming British settlers, the enslaved Africans made their escape into the hinterland.[5]

The British swiftly divided the island up and established sugar

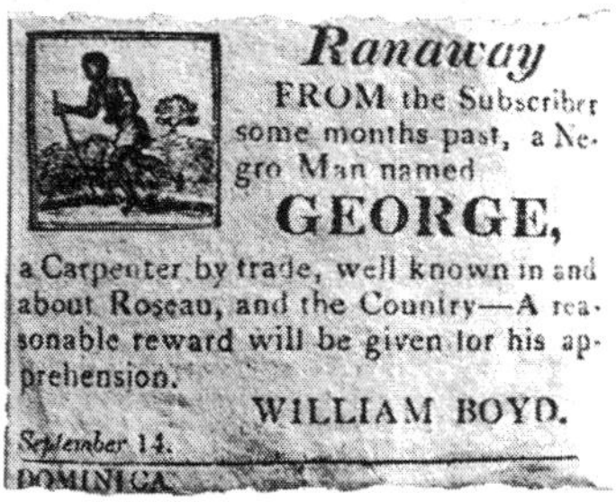

Ranaway
FROM the Subscriber some months past, a Negro Man named
GEORGE,
a Carpenter by trade, well known in and about Roseau, and the Country—A reasonable reward will be given for his apprehension.
WILLIAM BOYD.
September 14.
DOMINICA

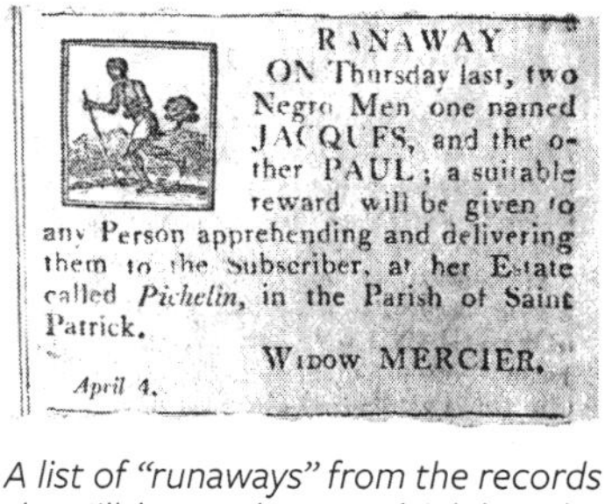

RANAWAY
ON Thursday last, two Negro Men one named JACQUES, and the other PAUL; a suitable reward will be given to any Person apprehending and delivering them to the Subscriber, at her Estate called *Pichelin*, in the Parish of Saint Patrick.
WIDOW MERCIER.
April 4.

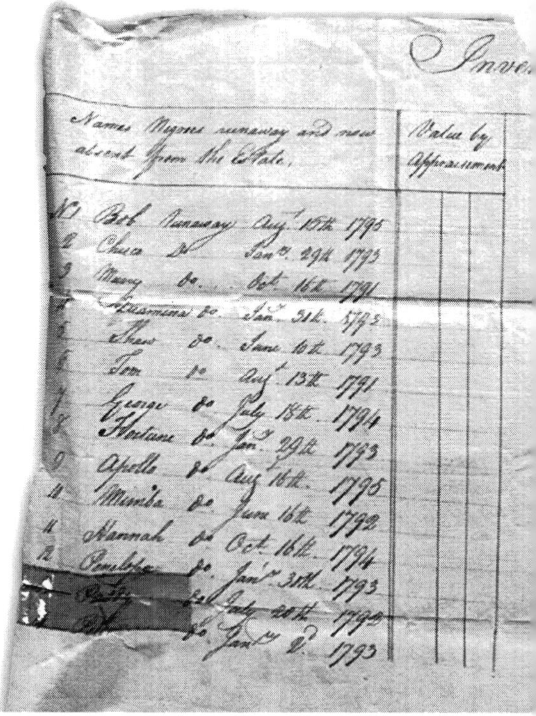

Inve[illegible]

Names Negroes runaway and now absent from the Estate	Value by Appraisement
1 Bob Runaway Aug 15th 1795	
2 Chica do Jan 29th 1793	
3 Mary do Oct 16th 1791	
4 [illegible] do Jan 31st 1793	
5 [illegible] do June 10th 1793	
6 Tom do Aug 13th 1791	
7 George do July 18th 1794	
8 Fontaine do Jan 29th 1793	
9 Apollo do Aug 16th 1795	
10 Minda do June 16th 1792	
11 Hannah do Oct 16th 1794	
12 [illegible] do Jan 30th 1793	
[illegible] do July 20th 1793	
[illegible] do Jan do 1793	

A list of "runaways" from the records of the Hillsborough estate (right) and notices from the Dominica Chronicle alerting the public to individual "runaways".

plantations so that Dominica became a society of slave labour in the manner of other - if richer - West Indian islands. This pattern of settlement replaced the more modest coffee estates of earlier French settlers, the *petit blancs* (small whites) from Martinique and Guadeloupe. But British tenure was brief, for in 1778 the French occupied the island installing the Marquis Duchilleau as governor. This was a significant development for the Maroons because Duchilleau appeared to have armed them with weapons taken from British residents as a means of consolidating French control.[6] The Maroons were thus transformed for a short while at least, from hunted fugitives to participants in power. And, boosted in confidence, they showed their dislike of the British by raiding their estates "with their conch shell blowing under French colours".[7]

However, French rule did not last and when the British returned in 1784 under the Treaty of Versailles, the Maroons kept up their attacks and showed their contempt for British offers of amnesty as the sometime chief judge of Dominica Thomas Atwood lamented: "To these proclamations the Maroons paid no manner of attention, but on the contrary they bid defiance to every measure..." They were free men and women living by their wits and their capacities in arms. They ran by their own rules. It is during this period that we see the emergence of powerful military chiefs and heads of well-organised camps. Their names still resonate: among them were Balla, Congoree, Pharcelle, Cicero, Jacko, Sandy, Coree-Greg, Mabouya, Noel, Louis Moco, Quashie and Elephant. Some - such as Jacko and Noel - spanned the whole period, their freedom lasting for more than 40 years. Many were African born.

During the First Maroon War (1785-90) the Maroons had adopted what might be a called a proto-nationalist stance to "extirpate" the English "dogs" from Dominica,[8] staging a series of raids on estates up and down the island - from Marigot, to Macoucherie, Mahaut to Rosalie. The British revenge ended with some of the chiefs, like Balla, being gibbeted alive, cut in pieces and decapitated.

By then, however, larger forces were at work. The world had been ushered into the modern epoch by the French Revolution in 1789. And to whom would its slogan of *Liberté, Fraternité, Egalité* appeal more keenly than to those held in slavery? The Haitian Revolution which followed in 1791, may itself have been sparked off by Maroon activity on that island. Coupled with this new political environment and the abolition of the slave trade in 1807 was the economic decline of the West Indian sugar barons, which left planters on islands in terminal decline.

In the same year as the Haitians launched their revolution came the New Year's Day revolt in Dominica. Lennox Honychurch, in his latest book "Negre Mawon: the Fighting Maroons of Dominica",[9] provides a detailed account of this day when the enslaved in the whole south-east of Dominica rose up in response to the revolutionary promptings of Henri Polinaire, a "free coloured" from Martinique who saw a chance to bring the revolution to the enslaved of Dominica. Polinaire has never been given his true place in the history of this island, and Honychurch's portrayal is a welcome start. It is to be hoped that Polinaire will one day take his place in the pantheon of greats who battled the evil of slavery in our part of the world, and so help to enrich our culture and understanding of our past.

The French continued to threaten British hold on Dominica until a failed attempt to take the island in 1805. After that the Maroons were on their own, but they showed themselves to be not simply the tools of the French but prosecutors in their own cause; and by the beginning of the second decade of the 19th century their attacks on economic targets had become a real threat to British colonial power.

The social, racial and colour hierarchy of plantation society determined that the whites were at the top. In Dominica, the French were sidelined when the British took over, and it was the British, a mediocre assortment of English, Scots and Irish, who controlled the legislative, executive and judicial institutions. This small, ramshackle group dominated a Council appointed by a Governor and an elected Assembly with executive power residing in the Governor appointed from London. In 1813 the population totalled 26,041 of whom 21,728 were enslaved, 1,325 were white and 2,988 were free persons of colour.[10] There were also deemed to be 800 runaways of whom nearly one half were women, while the Kalinago, by now squeezed

"The Negro Revenged", abolitionist image, which unusually shows a black man in a defiant gesture applauding the wrecking of a slave ship off shore. This print dates from 1807 when the Maroons of Dominica were building up their numbers and power.

into the north-eastern corner of the island, remained outside the jurisdiction of the British state.

The whites were divided by personal grudges and political infighting with no other purpose than maximum exploitation and oppression of African labour and the protection and maximisation of profits. They did, however, have a common enemy: the Maroons. As a Scottish doctor and slaver, William Bremner, put it in his unpublished memoirs: Dominica at that time was "torn by divisions in her internal politics, and... threatened by a growing enemy in her vitals, the daily accumulating hordes of runaway Negroes".[11]

It was at this point that Ainslie arrived in Dominica from Grenada where he had been lieutenant governor. What sort of man he was can be discerned from a complaint made against him by a free mulatto man in Grenada called Mitchel.[12] Ainslie had issued a proclamation requiring that all free people of colour take an oath of allegiance. Mitchel did exactly as the governor instructed and yet Ainslie ordered the poor man to be publicly

A view of Roseau, the capital of Dominica, surrounded by mountain ridges and peaks in the early 19th century.

flogged and then deported for no apparent reason. The abolitionist William Wilberforce referred the matter to the House of Commons in July 1814, but Ainslie escaped censure although his action was flagrantly unlawful.

Even a sympathiser, Sir Robert Heron MP, accused Ainslie, in the House of Commons, of drinking too much and of flogging four black soldiers in Dominica merely because they had failed to turn up on time.[13] Ainslie thought nothing of sending the decomposed head of one of his victims whom he had "tried" under an illegal court martial all the way across the island to be placed on a pike on an estate in Woodford Hill, unannounced and unrequested. Such gruesomeness marked a new low for a colonial slave regime.

Ainslie's friends in Dominica, in the Council, tried to defend him against the "public odium" he attracted, "as an oppressor of the slave, an enslaver of the free, as a contemner and violator of the laws, an abuser of his authority and an arbitrary, unfeeling tyrant"[14], but the records show that that was exactly what he was, a man who should have carried a health warning on his forehead instead of the governor's feathered hat. This is the man, however, who was appointed governor of Dominica with the power of life and death over captives whose original crime was none other than their membership of the African race.

In the months between his appointment and taking up his post, Ainslie must have familiarised himself with the Maroons and the past efforts to dislodge them and he resolved to deal with them. But he did not have the means to accomplish his objective, for the Militia, a force of local whites and mulattos appeared ineffectual. He had to create one. His secret weapon was a corps of Black Rangers, slaves recruited from the estates, and led by white officers. The Rangers would be fit enough to penetrate the forests and motivated enough by promises of freedom for killing a chief to do Ainslie's bidding. He eventually found his ideal commander in one Mr Savarin, whose surname still survives in the island, a lieutenant in the army with previous counter-Maroon experience.

The aim was to capture the Maroon camps in a three-pronged attack "to the windward from Rosalie, Tabery to Point Mulatre; in the centre of the island beyond the Layou and thirdly in the Colihaut Heights."[15] The objective was to turn the Maroon camps into permanent government garrisons so that the Maroons would be driven further and further into the mountain wastes where they would face the choice of death by starvation or surrender. That indeed is why so many of the maroons surrendered, especially in the wake of two hurricanes in 1813 which devastated their provision grounds.

Ainslie's strategy succeeded beyond all expectations. Between January and December 1814 all the major chiefs had either been killed or captured; one or two had surrendered. In all, 577 Maroons were either killed in the forests (18), captured or surrendered. On 7 February, Elephant was killed, Moko George on 20 April; Gabriel on 30 April and, in May 1814, Quashie was forced to surrender. On 12 July came the hardest blow of all for the Maroons when old Jacko was killed, intrepid to the last, killing three of his assailants before falling victim to the fourth, after 46 years on a ridge above the Layou River. The last major chief, Noel, was shot at the very end of 1814.

Ainslie's decision to eradicate the Maroons, and the unlawful methods he employed was one in which all sections of the slaving class, which included the Christian churches, the mulattos and whites, wholeheartedly concurred.[16] He was prepared to disregard or distort the law he was sworn to uphold in order to achieve his result. The legal authority for the trial of slaves derived from the Slave Act of 1788, but he paid scant regard to its provisions. While martial law in the West Indies at that time was "a wholly indispensable and legitimate facet of a colony's legal arsenal",[17] it appears there was no legal authority for Ainslie's courts martial, as was appreciated not only by two senior members of the legislature in Dominica but also - eventually - by Ainslie's superiors in London. The MP Robert Gordon concluded that Ainslie "appeared ignorant of colonial laws, and was unfit to be a governor"[18].

But there was a wider consideration. The controllers of the colonial state in London chose to concentrate on Ainslie's illegal conduct. But in truth the problem went much deeper; for it was not just Ainslie's behaviour that was in question but that of the legitimacy of the so-called law itself. For on what authority or justification did the British state claim to make a law that reduced people who had committed no wrong to slavery? Slavery was an act of unconscionable violence. In that regard, was it not pure hypocrisy to condemn an individual, like Ainslie, for violating the so-called law which was itself a violation of natural law? In this respect the edifice on which it was founded was an outrage committed by the state itself, from King and Parliament down to the last cruel racist like Ainslie who was sent to administer it.

It is no wonder that contempt was one of the noted reactions of the Maroons towards their torturers. The language of those involved in the system strained to take for granted notions of normality that the Maroons did not share. What passed for law was victors' justice, legitimate to those who wielded power, but not to the minds of the Maroons who confronted it and knew it for what it was – a violation of the law of conscience and of all that supported man's claim to be of a higher order than that of brutish beasts.

So what do the trial transcripts tell us? Their most notable feature seems to me to be the determination of the chief Maroons to fight on. Their contemptuous refusal to recognise the legitimacy of the British law did not escape their oppressors. That surely is a surprising state of affairs. Such contempt could not have been based on physical strength; it had to come from something more powerful – moral strength, for which the slavers had no answer.

We see this clearly in the story of Peter, from Hillsborough, who was charged and found guilty of "exciting a mutiny". On the morning of 5 January 1814, 22 slaves walked out of Hillsborough and refused to return until the manager was removed. The incident which sparked their complaint was the death of Frank, a fellow slave at Hillsborough, following a flogging. The men and women downed tools, walked to Roseau and took their complaint to the governor – intolerable behaviour in plantation society. When they refused to return to the estate, suspicion fell on Peter, "one of the most shrewd slaves on the estate", as being the leader of the plot and he was hauled before the courts martials' second sitting on the 16 January 1814.

He had deliberately led the Rangers on a wild-goose chase in spite of being offered "two heavy Joannases" (gold coins) to betray the whereabouts of Maroons, and he confronted his accusers with "no other answer than a contemptuous sneer"[19]. Peter was subsequently tried, but to his accusers he uttered not a word and to his interrogators, only that laconic sentence, "Your time is done now". His death assumed the quality of a sacrifice in which he called on his fellow African captives to take example on the manner of his passing.

Although the court recommended sparing Peter's life in the hope that he would serve as guide to the Rangers, as Moko George and Apollo did after him, Ainslie, as bloodthirsty as ever, insisted on execution and that "the head to be cut off and put on a pike in the market place, the body to be hung in chains on Hillsborough estate".[20]

The contempt that Peter showed towards his captors was not unique. Ainslie had found this out to his astonishment: one former Maroon whom he had sent to carry his proclamation (essentially to say surrender or die) to Quashie, a leading Maroon chief, was executed. When Ainslie put a bounty of 1000 dollars on Quashie's head; Quashie doubled it - for Ainslie's head. As Thomas Atwood observed a generation earlier, the Maroons in "deriding the attempt at reducing them by force, threatened to do still greater mischief".[21]

Another notable feature of the trials is the complex relationship that existed between the Maroons and the plantation. Even at the heart of the plantation society itself the Maroons maintained a vibrant market in goods. The evidence in the trials details how the Maroons would visit the estates equipped with the products of the forest such as wahwah (an indigenous wild yam) and crapauds (edible frogs) and would exchange them for useful - and vital - items such as salt and saltfish, guns and ammunition.

The transcripts of the courts martial of Victor and Joe, for example, show that Maroons were accustomed to visiting their allies on the estates under the very noses of the planters. Victor, for example, was charged with "having supplied the runaways with gunpowder, saltfish and tobacco", convicted and hanged. In the evidence of a witness and self-confessed former Maroon called Papynard, we learn that Victor's house was a regular contact point for the Maroons, who left their guns there when they went to town. Joe, who was hanged for "harbouring and supplying the runaway slaves" and who belonged "to the estate of Cubbin", was another such point of contact. He received parties of Maroons - as the witness Marie Jeanne put it, "Great many. They came every Friday" - and traded in wahwah for items such as salt and tobacco which Joe purchased in Roseau on behalf of the "runaways" while they waited at his house on the estate.

The trials must have opened the planters' eyes to the deep network that the Maroons had forged within the very confines of their unfreedom, thus confirming that marronage undermined the institution of slavery and would always pose a risk to it.

But no one who seeks to understand the culture of the people of the island can ignore the Maroons' contribution, just as it would be unthinkable to underestimate the abiding influence of Kalinago culture on

Dominica. The Maroons gave the lie to the pretences of the white slavers that the "Negro" was born inferior and ignorant of the higher qualities that inspire men to die for freedom. They also recognised that the system of government and society imposed on them was based on naked force and had to be confronted. They thus set in train a tradition in Dominica that ensures that abuse of governmental power can be challenged by direct action of the people. Concomitant with this is an independence of spirit and a combative assertion of equality which to this day can test organisational discipline to the core. The commemoration of the 200th anniversary of the death of Chief Jacko on 12 July 1814, together with recent publications on the Maroons, show the strength of their legacy. There is also a proposal to create a monument in the form of a perpetual flame in their memory and to reconstruct the sites of Maroon camps as places of interest, education and edification, for both the nation and visitors.

In the epilogue of Hugh Thomas' book, The Slave Trade, he wrote, "The slave remains an unknown warrior invoked by moralists on both sides of the Atlantic, recalled now in museums in one-time slave ports from Liverpool to Elmina, but all the same unspeaking, and therefore remote and elusive." It is the power of the trial transcripts in this book that the enslaved become a little less remote, a little less unspeaking as we listen to the voices of the men and women who were so intimately involved in the dramatic events of those days and who suffered so much for their right to be free.

Bernard Wiltshire

George Ainslie, Governor of Dominica 1813-1814, issued the first of his proclamations (below) telling the Maroons in May 1813 to surrender or die. Right: spirit of resistance - "A cudgelling match between English and French Negroes" by Agostino Brunias, who painted scenes of Dominica in the 1760s.

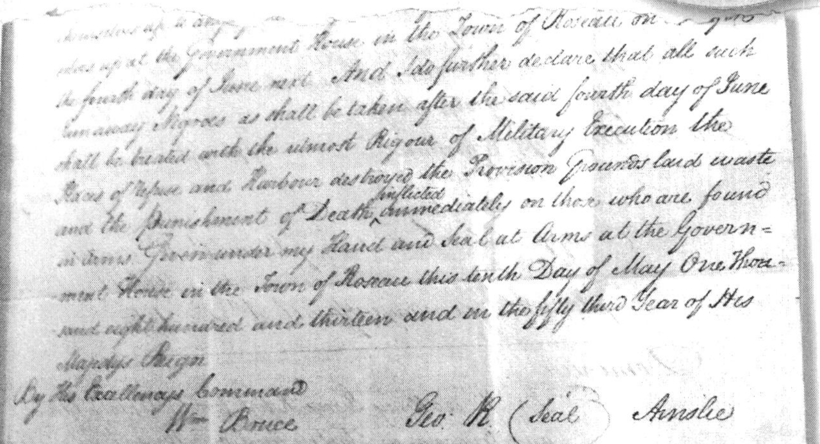

surrender up to any ... Government House in the Town of Roseau on ...
... up at the Government House in the Town of Roseau on ... before
the fourth day of June next And I do further declare that all such
Runaway Negroes as shall be taken after the said fourth day of June
shall be treated with the utmost Rigour of Military Execution the
Places of Refuge and Harbour destroyed the Provision Grounds laid waste
and the Punishment of Death inflicted immediately on those who are found
in Arms. Given under my Hand and Seal at Arms at the Government House in the Town of Roseau this tenth Day of May One Thousand eight hundred and thirteen and in the fifty third Year of His
Majesty's Reign

By His Excellency's Command
Wm. Bruce
Secretary

Geo: R. (Seal) Ainslie
Governor & Brig. General

filed in the Secretary's Office the 10th Day of May 1813.

1813
Suppression of the Maroons begins

By 1813, the forests of Dominica were home to at least 800 Maroons living as free men and women in self-regulating communities away from the tyranny of the estates. In collaboration with the enslaved, they had become a serious threat to the economic and social wellbeing of colonial life: not only had their numbers increased, but there had been attacks on plantations, killings, robberies in Roseau, and owners driven from their estates. Sixty slaves from Castle Bruce estate, for example, had left the previous year, and the rest, according to estate attorney James Clarke, were "in such a state of insubordination as to have refused to obey the manager's orders, and to have it in contemplation to join those already absent".[1] All over the island, plantations were in ferment as more and more of the enslaved took to camps in the wilderness of the island's hinterland.

The small governing class of white men bickered among themselves over the crumbs of privilege, imposed their racially-defined rights, often brutally, over the enslaved and struggled to stay out of debt. One thing, however, united them: their fear and loathing of a common enemy, the "daily accumulating hordes"[2], the runaways, as they were disparagingly known, or the Maroons (Negs Mawons in French Creole) and their allies on the estates. The whites thought the Maroons were on the verge of massacre and insurrection. "Such a plan was certainly formed" was how a group of planters and merchants saw it.[3]

Earlier strategies to quell the Maroons had failed but all that changed with the arrival of a new governor, Major General George Robert Ainslie, in April 1813. Negotiation, which had occasionally been a feature of Maroon activity since the 1770s, was not an option for Ainslie, a man who appeared to be driven by repressive and brutal impulses. He wasted no time in adopting new strategies to destroy the Maroons. His policy was surrender or die.

17 APRIL 1813

George Ainslie (1776-1839) arrived in Dominica on 17 April as governor succeeding Sir Edward Barnes, ten months after his appointment on 1 June 1812. Born in Scotland, Ainslie had had an undistinguished military career until, through personal connections, he shifted into a diplomatic life. He was briefly Lieutenant Governor of Grenada (1812-1813) where his intemperate (and illegal) behaviour would draw comments in the British press and in parliament - but by then he had been appointed to a better paid and more prestigious job in Dominica. The Examiner, a radical weekly newspaper in England, described his humiliating departure from Grenada: "Instead of being followed to the shore by a grateful and applauding multitude... he was merely accompanied and guarded, as it were, by a few menials and satellites, the people looking on with high satisfaction at his departure, and expressing their contempt of him by repeated hissings."[4]

But it appears he was welcomed in Dominica. Soon after his arrival, William Bremner, a Scottish doctor, member of the governing Council, planter and estate attorney, wrote in his memoirs that it was clear that the new governor would act vigorously against the Maroons.

> Gov. A [Ainslie] appears very early after assuming the government to have been aware of the necessity of adopting means for suppressing these hordes of runaways, against whom, though so often represented as most dangerous to the safety of the colony, no effectual steps had for a long time been taken... It was reserved for Gov. A to view the danger in its proper light, and at last to adopt a plan which has nearly eradicated the evil. (WB, p140)

10 MAY 1813

With the Maroons in the ascendancy, Ainslie issued the first of his infamous "proclamations". Adopting a policy of carrot and stick - amnesty on the one hand and punishment on the other - Ainslie threatened the Maroons with death unless they surrendered: and then to be returned to their owners. This set the tone for the rest of his administration in Dominica. News of the proclamations would eventually reach the ears of the British political establishment and it was this and subsequent developments which set in motion Ainslie's eventual recall to England. By that time, however, his campaign to eradicate the Maroons and their social, economic and military networks and camps had been achieved. Here is Ainslie's first proclamation.

> Whereas several Negroes have under different pretences absented themselves from their masters' service and whereas if a free and unconditional pardon were offered to such runaway slaves [that] might return to their duty I do therefore by this my proclamation offer a free and unconditional pardon to all such runaways who return to their duty and deliver themselves up to the magistrates of this colony or surrender themselves up to Government House in the town of Roseau on or before the 4th day of June next, where their grievances will meet with every proper consideration. And I do further declare that all such runaways that shall be taken after the 4th day of June shall be treated with the utmost vigour of military execution, their[?] places of refuge and harbours destroyed, their provision grounds laid waste and the punishment of death inflicted on those who are found in arms. (CO 71/49)

1 JUNE 1813

Before the deadline of 4 June expired, Ainslie issued another proclamation - with the same promises and threats - and extended the deadline to 1 July. This was to ensure, according to Ainslie, that the proclamation reached the ears of the Maroons in all the camps. Ainslie later told his boss Lord Bathurst, the Secretary of State for War and the Colonies, that he had even sent messengers to the camps, with the proclamation "couched in language the fugitives could understand"[5] to help publicise his amnesty. But this tactic misfired when Ainslie sent one emissary, a slave who had recently surrendered, to the camp of Quashie, a chief. Quashie had the unfortunate messenger tried, and shot. Then, when Ainslie set a price of one thousand dollars for the head of Quashie, the chief doubled the price for the Governor's head.[6] This confrontation between a Maroon chief and an imperial governor became one of the iconic moments of this period, sometimes known as the Second Maroon War, which ended in 1814.

THE COURTS OF SPECIAL SESSIONS

The first defendants under Ainslie's pugilistic regime were brought to trial at a court of special sessions on 17 July. These men and women were both Maroons and the enslaved on the estates. Most were charged with being "runaways" or assisting the "runaways". The support given to the Maroons in the forests by the enslaved was key to the Maroons' survival. It is relevant to note that the punishments - execution, flogging and banishment - given to those who assisted the runaways were as severe as for those convicted for being runaways.

Under the revised Slave Act of 1793, the law "for the protection and better governance of slaves" directed that all slaves accused of running away, harbouring or supplying runaways, and other capital crimes, should be tried by a court of special sessions, composed of three justices and a jury of six men. Special sessions were usually heard six times a year, but in 1813 and 1814 more sittings than usual were held.

The judiciary for such courts comprised Justices of the Peace, the Provost Marshal (similar to a sheriff), the Attorney General, a clerk and a jury of six white men, one of whom was chosen from among the six to act as foreman. The Justices of the Peace were laymen, drawn from Dominica's small and undistinguished white establishment. Most of them were also members of the island's executive and legislative bodies and occupied these roles at the same time as being JPs. Among the JPs for this trial, for example, were John Gordon and William Anderson, both, at various times speakers of the House of Assembly, and Charles Bertrand, a member of the House of Assembly.

The slave defendants had no legal representation. There was no public defender.[7] *Slave legislation was designed to confirm the status of slaves as property and reflected the interests of the slave-owning class and the slave system itself: "The primary function of the British West India slave laws was either directly or indirectly repressive."*[8] *Law was based on fear.*

These court records suggest that the trials were perfunctory. They do not, for example, provide any details of the prosecution's case nor, indeed, of that of the defence. All the defendants are recorded as having pleaded "not guilty". Of the 32 defendants tried between July and December 1813, three were sentenced to death, of whom one died in jail. (CO 71/51)

17 JULY 1813
The TRIALS of CALISTE, ANGELLE, GUILLAUME, DUNDAS and TOUSSAINT

At a court of special sessions held for the said island on Saturday the 17th day of July 1813. Present: John Gordon, Charles Bertrand and William Anderson Esquires (Justices of the Peace), Thomas Hayes (acting clerk of the Session), Edward H Beech (acting Provost Marshall) and William Webb Glanville[9] Esquire (Attorney General).

CALISTE and **ANGELLE**, two Negro slaves belonging to Mr Warner, stand charged with having had intercourse[10] and correspondence with the runaway Negroes, by receiving into their house John, a runaway Negro belonging to Mrs Nibbs, and sundry other runaway slaves unknown. The said Caliste and Angelle having been charged with the said indictment pleaded "not guilty" whereupon a jury having been empanelled by the Provost Marshal and duly sworn, to wit James Matthews, Henry Nesbit, Edward Hughes, Maurice Ogston, Charles Miller and John Bennett who made choice of James Matthews as the foreman, and the evidence on the behalf of the prosecution as well as on behalf of the prisoners having been heard, the jurors pronounced by their foreman that the prisoners are guilty of harbouring runaways but recommend them to the mercy of the court as no proof appeared that the prisoners knew the said slaves so harboured to be runaways.

GUILLAUME, a Negro slave, the property of A and N Moreau, stands charged with having the 14th day of May last struck Thomas Carter, the overseer, on the plantation of the said A and N Moreau, he then and there being a white person, with a cutlass giving the said Thomas Carter a cut across the nose, whereupon the prisoner having been charged with the said indictment pleaded "not guilty", whereupon a jury, having been empanelled by the Provost Marshal, that is to say James Alexander Laborie, Isaac Atkinson, Balthazar Blanc, Thomas Reeves, William Wright and Brunton Murat and having made choice of James Alexander Laborie as their foreman were duly sworn, and the evidence adduced on behalf of the prosecution as well as on behalf of the prisoner having been heard, pronounced by their foreman that the prisoner is guilty.

DUNDAS, a Negro slave belonging to Goodwill estate, stands charged that on or about the month of May 1810 he attempted to force a woman named Franky between the mill cases whilst the mill was going about, and that in the month of July following he stabbed the driver on the said estate with a bayonet, that he afterwards ran away and was absent for a year. The prisoner being charged with the said indictment pleaded "not guilty" whereupon a jury having been empanelled by the Provost Marshal to wit James Alexander Laborie, Isaac Atkinson, Balthazar Blanc, Thomas Reeves, William Wright and Brunton Murat and having made choice of

A FORCIBLE APPEAL for the ABOLITION of the SLAVE TRADE

Flogging the enslaved in the West Indies. Flogging was a common punishment - up to 100 lashes - dispensed by the courts during the Maroon trials.

James Alexander Laborie as their foreman were duly sworn and the evidence against the prisoner having been heard as well as the evidence adduced on his behalf having been fully heard pronounced by their foreman that the prisoner is "guilty".

TOUSSAINT, a Negro slave belonging to the heir of John Powell deceased (here William Anderson Esquire retired from the bench he being the attorney to the heir of the said John Powell, and the Honourable James Clark took his seat on the bench in his place), stands charged with having practised witchcraft. He was remanded to jail for further evidence. The court adjourned until the 19th instant. (CO 71/51)

The verdicts for these defendants (except for that of Toussaint, whose fate is unknown) were given two days later, on 19 July 1813. Caliste and Guillaume were sentenced to death (Caliste was to die in jail) while the two other defendants were "banished for life". Banishment - apart from execution and flogging - was a favourite judicial punishment for the enslaved in the British West Indies. It served two purposes: it was a way to get rid of troublemakers and also provided a source of labour for new imperial pastures, at this time often in Trinidad and the Guianas. In Dominica, the state probably paid compensation to the owners while the convicted slaves were put on boats to be sold elsewhere - never to return.

CALISTE and **ANGELLE**, two Negro slaves belonging to Mrs Warner, found guilty at the last court were brought up for judgement (here the Honourable James Clark came into court and took his seat) whereupon the court proceeded to pass the following sentences on the prisoners. Caliste by directing that he be taken from the place where he now stands to the place from whence he came and from thence to the place of execution and ***to be hung by the neck until he be dead***, at such time as his Excellency the Governor shall be pleased to appoint, and the court pronounced sentence on the prisoner Angelle that she be remanded to jail until she can be banished from the island.

GUILLAUME, belonging to A and N Moreau, being brought up, the court proceeded to pass sentence of the law by ordering that the prisoner be taken to the place from whence he came from there to the place of execution, there ***to be hung by the neck until he be dead*** at such time as His Excellency the Governor shall please to appoint.

DUNDAS found guilty at the last court was brought up and ordered to be banished for life. (CO 71/51)

13 AUGUST 1813
The TRIALS of CHANCE, JOHNSON, QUASHEE, ETIENNE and BUOY

The courts of special sessions resumed three weeks after a terrible hurricane struck the island on 23 July. Ainslie made a request to London for supplies, fresh provisions, lumber, shingles, and reported devastation and famine as well as deaths among the regular British soldiers stationed above Roseau on Morne Bruce. The Council minutes record that the troops were "totally unfit for service".[11] Key buildings such as Government House and the Court House were also destroyed.

At this trial, Edward Beech, the acting Provost Marshal, is named as a translator/interpreter. This reflects the colonial linguistic divisions on the island between French and English. Although British rule had been in place - with interruptions - since 1763, the French planters and their slaves, usually on coffee estates, occupied a separate cultural and linguistic place in Dominican society.

At a court of special sessions held for the said island at the court house in the town of Roseau on Friday the 13 August 1813. Present the Honourable Archibald Gloster, George Garraway and James Johnston Esquires (Justices of the Peace), William Webb Glanville Esquire (Attorney General), Thomas Hayes (acting clerk of the court), Edward H Beech (acting Provost Marshal and interpreter and translator).

CHANCE, JOHNSON and **QUASHEE,** three Negro slaves belong to Canefield estate, stand charged with having left the estate with an intent to run away and of disobeying the orders of the manager in not turning out to work when ordered. Johnson was ordered by the court to be recommitted to gaol, no jury being necessary under the Slave Act. In the trial of Chance and Quashee, the court were pleased after hearing the evidence on both sides to order Chance to receive 39 lashes on the bare breech in the market place and Quashee 25 lashes in the same manner and place.

ETIENNE, a Negro slave belonging to Mistress Moreau, stands charged with having at different times given salt and other provisions and necessaries to the runaway slaves contrary to an Act of this island in such case made and provided, and with having broken open an outhouse belonging to the estate and with having taken therefrom salt and butter contrary to the Act in such cases made and provided, whereupon the prisoner having been charged with his indictment pleaded "not guilty" and a jury having been empanelled by the Provost Marshal to wit Robert Merritt, Thomas Ralph, Francis Culpeper, Frederick Garraway, Edward Preston and Thomas Rawsthorn and having made choice of Robert Merritt as their foreman were duly sworn and the evidence adduced on behalf of the prosecution as well as on behalf of the prisoner having been fully heard pronounced by their foreman that the prisoner is "not guilty"; the prisoner was therefore ordered to be discharged.

Morne Neg Mawon (Maroon Mountain) shows a classic Dominican landscape, one ideal for Maroon communities.

BUOY, a Negro slave the property of Mistress Foye, stands charged with having absented from the service of his owner for upwards of six months prior to her commitment contrary to an Act of this island in such case made and provided and also with having broken open the dwelling house of the said Mistress Foye situated in the parish of St Peter and Island aforesaid with an intent to steal therefrom, contrary to an Act of this island in such case made and provided, the said prisoner having been charged with this indictment pleaded "not guilty" whereupon a jury having been empanelled by the Provost Marshal to wit Robert Merritt, Thomas Ralph, Francis Culpeper, Frederick Garraway, Edward Preston and Thomas Rawsthorn and having made choice of Robert Merritt as their foreman were duly sworn, and the evidence adduced on behalf of the prosecution as well as on behalf of the prisoner having been fully heard pronounced by their foreman that the prisoner is "guilty" whereupon the court proceeded to pronounce the sentence of the law by ordering that [the] prisoner be taken from the place from whence he came and from thence to the usual place of execution there ***to be hung by the neck until he be dead*** at such time as his Excellency the Governor shall appoint. (CO 71/51)

28 SEPTEMBER 1813
The TRIALS of FRANK, BILLY, SALESTINE, SAMPSON, CHARLES, JACK, JOHNSON, JOHN, CUFFY TOBY, JOACINTHE and HARRY

A court of special sessions sat again, one month after another hurricane had hit the island. At this point Ainslie described Dominica as "ill-fated".[12] *Hurricanes undermined not just the institutions of the state but also the capacity of the runaways to survive: with their homes and provision grounds destroyed, and their hiding places exposed, they were physically if not mentally weakened.*[13]

However, it was not just the weather that delayed the judicial process. On occasions, there appear to have been delays in hearing cases either because the Justices of the Peace did not turn up or, as in this case, because the evidence was not available. Earlier that September, the House of the Assembly minutes record that William

Wright, the manager of Salisbury estate, had four times travelled to Roseau (some ten miles away) to give evidence against a Maroon and that each time no court had been formed to try him. "Every time he [Wright] has been so called to town he has been under the necessity of bringing with him four able Negroes from their work on the estate as boatmen (his state of health not allowing him to ride)."[14] Governor Ainslie would use the delays in these hearings to justify his holding of courts martial.[15]

Court of special sessions held in Roseau, Monday 28 September 1813. Present: the Honourable Robert Reid and the Honourable William Bremner, William Anderson and Alexander Fraser Esquires (Justices of the Peace), William Webb Glanville Esquire (Attorney General), Thomas Hayes (acting clerk of the Crown), Edward H Beech (acting Provost Marshal and interpreter and translator).

FRANK, a Negro slave belonging to Eusebe Serrant, and committed as a runaway on the 2nd day of April last, was ordered by the court to be discharged, no evidence being produced to connect him of the crime laid to his charge.

BILLY, a Negro slave belonging to Mr Laroque, charged with being a runaway was ordered by the court to be recommitted to gaol until further evidence.

SALESTINE, a Negro slave belonging to Beriqua estate, stands charged with having absented himself from his owner's employ for upwards of six months contrary to the Act of this island in such case made and provided, the prisoner having been charged with the said indictment and pleaded not guilty whereupon a jury having been empanelled by the Provost Marshal to wit Robert Merritt, Frederick Garraway, George Anderson, John Howell, Edward Preston and Thomas Secker and having made choice of Robert Merritt as the foreman were duly sworn and the evidence adduced on behalf of the Prosecution as well as on the behalf of the prisoner having been fully heard pronounced by their foreman that the prisoner is "guilty" whereupon the court ordered the prisoner to be remanded to gaol until an opportunity offered of banishment from the island.

SAMPSON, a Negro slave belonging to the estate of Laronde, committed as a runaway on the 20th day of August last was ordered by the court to be remanded to gaol for further evidence and the Marshal was directed to summon the owner of the said slave to attend with the evidence at the next court.

CHARLES, a Negro slave belonging to Mr Marceau, stands charged with having absented himself from his owner's employ for upwards of six months contrary to an Act of this island in such case made and provided; the prisoner having been charged with the said indictment pleaded "not guilty" whereupon the aforesaid jury having been duly sworn and the evidence adduced, on behalf of the prosecution as well as on behalf of the prisoner, having been fully heard, pronounced by their foreman that the prisoner is "guilty" whereupon the court ordered that the prisoner should be detained in custody of the Marshal until an opportunity offered to banish from the island.

JACK, a Negro slave belonging to Mrs Nibbs, committed on the 15th day of July last as a runaway was brought, was ordered to be remanded for further evidence and the Marshal was ordered to summon the owner of the said slave to attend with his evidence at the next court.

JOHNSON, a Negro slave belonging to Canefield estate, committed on the 2nd day of August as a runaway was remanded to gaol, three out of the four justices on the bench being joint attorneys for that property, he was ordered to be brought up at the next court.

JOHN and **CUFFY**, Negro slaves belonging to Hillsboro estate (here the Honourable Mr Bremner retired from the Bench being an attorney to the said estate), stand charged with having absented themselves from the employ of their owner for upwards of six months contrary to an act of this island in such case made and provided the prisoners having been charged with this indictment pleaded "not guilty" and the aforesaid jury having been empanelled by the Provost Marshal and having chosen Robert Merritt for their foreman were duly sworn, and the evidence adduced against the prisoners as well as that on their behalf having been fully heard pronounced by their foreman that the prisoners are "guilty"

> whereupon the court ordered that the said prisoners be remanded to gaol until they can be banished the island, but it appeared in evidence that the said slaves voluntarily surrendered themselves and from other circumstances in their favour, which also appeared, the court requested that His Excellency the Governor might be informed thereof in mitigation of the sentence. (CO 71/51)

3 OCTOBER 1813

At the beginning of October, Ainslie issued his third proclamation concluding with an even more violently phrased threat against those runaways who did not surrender.

> Whereas detachments of his Majesty's Troops have been sent into the woods and have destroyed the tracks of the runaways camps. And whereas I am desirous of affording the misguided slaves who have absented themselves from the employ of their owners an opportunity of returning to their duty before I proceed to extremities, I do, by this my proclamation offer a free and unconditional pardon to all runaway slaves who shall surrender themselves at the Government House in the town of Roseau on or before the 24th day of this month of October; and I do

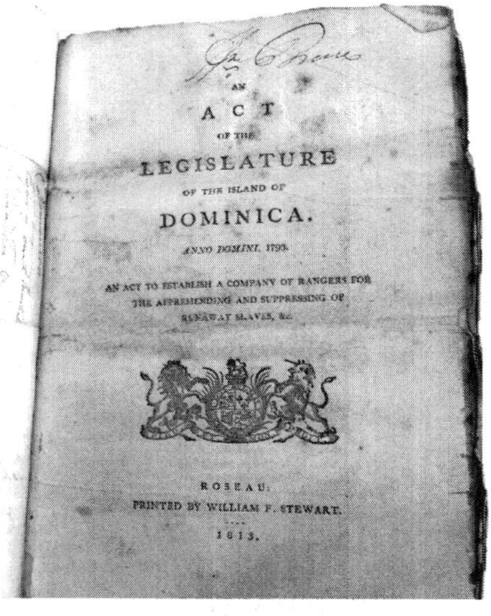

AN
ACT
OF THE
LEGISLATURE
OF THE ISLAND OF
DOMINICA.
ANNO DOMINI, 179[illegible]
AN ACT TO ESTABLISH A COMPANY OF RANGERS FOR THE APPREHENDING AND SUPPRESSING OF RUNAWAY SLAVES, &c.
ROSEAU:
PRINTED BY WILLIAM F. STEWART.
1813.

"An Act to establish a company of Rangers for the apprehending and suppressing of runaway slaves". The Rangers became an effective weapon in the destruction of the Maroons.

further declare that the utmost rigour of military execution shall be put in force against all those runaway slaves that may be apprehended after that period neither age nor sex spared, all indiscriminately will be put to the bayonet. (CO 71/49)

On 13 October, three of the slaves remanded from the last sitting were again brought before the court for sentencing; three other slaves were also charged.

At a court of special sessions holden for the said island at the Court House in Roseau, the 13th day of October 1813. Present: the Honourable Archibald Gloster, James Clark and Robert Garraway, George Garraway Esquires (Justices of the Peace), William Webb Glanville (Attorney General), Thomas Hayes (acting clerk of the Crown), Edward H Beech (acting Provost Marshal and interpreter).

BILLY, a Negro slave belonging to Mr Laroque, stands charged with having been runaway upwards of seven years, the said Negro having been found "guilty", he was sentenced by the court to be banished the island.
SAMPSON, a Negro slave belonging to Mr Laronde, stands charged with having runaway upwards of three years and a half, the prisoner having been found "guilty", he was sentenced by the court to be banished the island.
HARRY, a Negro slave belonging to Mr Courché, and **JOACINTHE**, a Negro slave belonging to Mr Sablon, stand charged as being runaways and as leader of bands of runaways in the woods. The prisoner Harry having been found "guilty", the court sentenced him to be banished the island; Joacinthe having been found "not guilty" was ordered by the court to be discharged.
JACK, a Negro slave belonging to Mrs Nibbs, stands charged with having runaway above six months, the prisoner having been found "not guilty" the court ordered him to be discharged.
TOBY, a Negro slave belonging to Doctor Greenaway, stands charged with having run away upwards of eight months, the prisoner having been found "guilty" the court ordered him to be banished the island. (CO 71/51)

William Bremner commented on the success of the Governor's campaign although he noted that the majority of the runaways who had surrendered were women and children and that the "most bloody chiefs" were still holding out.

> Scarcely a week passed over without their bringing in parties, sometimes amounting to 20, of the renegades, so that in the course of a few months nearly 200 had been taken, and a greater number had surrendered. It was observed notwithstanding, that the majority of these were women and children, and that even up to the month of November some of the principal and most bloody chiefs, vizt., Apollo, Noel and Louis Moco, continued obstinately to hold out. (WB, p162)

12 NOVEMBER 1813
The TRIALS of JEAN PIERRE, FRANCOIS, CHARLES, CALAIS, BILLY, TOBY and CHARLES

Dominica. At a court of special sessions holden for the said island at the court house in Roseau the 12th day of November 1813. Present: the Honourable Benjamin Lucas, Robert Reid and John Gordon Esquires (Justices of the Peace), David F Rand (acting Attorney General), Thomas Hayes (acting clerk of the Crown), Edward H Beech (acting Provost Marshal and interpreter).

JEAN PIERRE, a Negro slave belonging to Madame Durour Beltgens, stands charged as having run away. He was remanded to gaol by the court for further evidence and the Marshal was ordered to summon his owner to attend with her witnesses at the next court.

FRANCOIS, a Negro slave belonging to Madame Michineau, stands charged with being a runaway, the prisoner was remanded to gaol for further evidence, and the Marshal was directed to summon his owner to attend with her witnesses at the next court.

CHARLES, a Negro slave belonging to Bell Hill estate, stands charged with being a runaway. He was ordered to be remanded to gaol until the next court for evidence.

CALAIS, belonging to Madame Michineau, **BILLY** belonging to York Valley estate, **TOBY** belonging to Canefield estate and **CHARLES** belonging to Macouchery estate, severally stand charged with being runaways, were remanded back to gaol for further evidence and ordered to be brought up next court.

25 NOVEMBER 1813
The TRIALS of JEAN PIERRE, ETIENNE, MINGO, MAGDELANE and JOHNSON

Dominica. At a court of special sessions held at the court house in Roseau and Island aforesaid the 25th day of November 1813. Present: the Honourable James Clark, John Gordon and George Garraway Esquires (Justices of the Peace).

JEAN PIERRE, a Negro slave the property of Durour Beltgens, stands charged with having run away from his owner's employ upwards of six months, the jury having found the prisoner "guilty", the court sentenced him to be banished the island agreeable to the 13th clause of the Slave Act. **ETIENNE**, a Negro slave the property of Mr Lockhart, stands charged with having run away from his owner's employ upwards of six months. The prisoner was remanded in gaol for further evidence until the next court. **MINGO**, a Negro slave belonging to Madame Scipio, **MAGDELANE**, a Negro slave the property of Doctor Spencer; and **JOHNSON** a Negro slave belonging to Canefield estate, severally stand charged with having been run away from their owner's employ for upwards of six months contrary to the Act regd, the jury having found all the prisoners "guilty" the court ordered them to be banished according to law.

9 DECEMBER 1813
The TRIALS of ETIENNE, CALISTE, SIMEON, TIM and LAWSA

This sitting of the special sessions produced a mixture of verdicts: two defendants were found not guilty, two had their cases dismissed, one for being of "miserable and wretched appearance" and one was found guilty.

At a court of special sessions held for the said island at the court house in Roseau the 9th day of December 1813. Present: the Honourable Archibald Gloster, Robert Reid, and Robert Garraway, David F Rand (acting Attorney General), Thomas Hayes (acting clerk of the Crown), Edward H Beech (acting Provost Marshal and interpreter).

ETIENNE, a Negro slave belonging to Mr Lockhart, stands charged with having held intercourse and correspondence with the Runaway slaves contrary to an act of this island in such case made and provided, the prisoner having been charged with this indictment pleaded "not guilty" whereupon a jury having been empanelled by the Provost Marshal to wit Robert Merritt, John Dodds, John Cubbin, Thomas Secker, Peter Monboucher and Alexander Dunbar, and having made choice of Robert Merritt as their foreman were duly sworn and the evidence adduced on behalf of the prosecution as well as on behalf of the prisoner having been fully heard pronounced by their foreman that the prisoner is "guilty", whereupon the court sentenced the prisoner to be banished the island.

CALISTE, a Negro man belonging to Mr Renault, charged with being a runaway was ordered to be released by the court, no evidence appearing against him.

SIMEON, a Negro man belonging to Grand Frere, stands charged with having sold, given or bartered firearms, cutlasses and rum to the runaway slaves contrary to an Act of this island in such case made and provided, and also with having held intercourse and correspondence with the runaway slaves contrary to the Act in such case made and provided, the prisoner having been charged with this indictment pleaded "not guilty", whereupon a jury having been duly sworn and the evidence adduced on behalf of the prosecution as well as on behalf of the prisoner having been fully heard pronounced by their foreman that the prisoner is "not guilty" whereupon the prisoner was discharged.

TIM, a Negro slave belonging to Mr Arnaud, stands charged with having held intercourse and correspondences with the runaway slaves contrary to the Act in such case made and provided, the prisoner having been

> charged with this indictment pleaded "not guilty" whereupon a jury having been duly sworn and the evidence adduced on behalf of the prosecution as well as on behalf of the prisoner having been fully heard pronounced by their foreman that the prisoner is "not guilty" whereupon the prisoner was discharged.
>
> **LAWSA**, a Negro slave belonging to Mr Noble, stands charged with having absented himself from his owner's employ for near six months, from his miserable and wretched appearance the court were induced to order him to be dismissed.

Despite Ainslie's success in bringing Maroons to trial Bremner thought that the white population remained jittery, anticipating an attack on Roseau, where, says Bremner, guns were planted "at every avenue of the town to oppose them".

> The insolence, depredations and outrages of the runaways continued daily to increase, and their numbers rapidly to multiply by continual desertions from the estates. An alarm was indeed excited one day, that a great body of them in arms were close at hand, approaching to attack the town of Roseau, and so general was the belief of their being capable of such an attempt, that the whole garrison and Militia were called out by the Government and guns planted at every avenue of the town to oppose them. Women and children were seen flying to get on board ship to avoid falling into the hands of the savages, which they apprehended. It was soon discovered indeed that this alarm was without foundation, but the terror it excited for a time was sufficient to show the light in which the strength of the runaways was generally estimated. And indeed the spirits of insubordination became so plainly apparent among the whole slave population that no doubt could be entertained that if some efficient measures were not speedily adopted to quell those hordes, our lives and properties were placed in the most imminent danger. (WB, pp143-144)

While, by the end of 1813, Ainslie's policies had brought 30 men and two women to trial, his most repressive strategy was to come.

Steep and narrow, the Jacko Steps, could only be approached by attackers slowly and in single file. Inset: now visitors are directed to them.

1814
Up against martial law

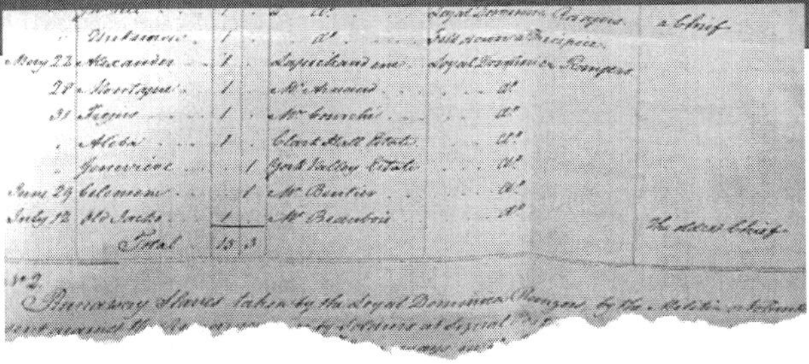

	Vulcan	1		do	Fell down a Precipice	
May 22	Alexander	1		Lapuchand ...	Loyal Dominica Rangers	
28	Mortigue	1		Mr Armand	do	
31	Jaques	1		Mr Granche	do	
	Alede	1		Black Hall Estate	do	
	Genevieve		1	York Valley Estate	do	
June 29	Celemene		1	Mr Bertier	do	
July 12	Mr Jacko	1		Mr Beaubois	do	The oldest Chief
	Total	13	3			

N°2

Runaway Slaves taken by the Loyal Dominica Rangers, by the ...

Right: recording Jacko's death, 12 July 1814, with the comment, "the oldest chief".

Above: the Market House on the Bay Front, Roseau, where the courts martial of 1814 took place. It forms one boundary with the market place, the scene of executions.

With Governor Ainslie's declaration of martial law - the suspension of civilian rule - in January 1814 and the start of courts martial in the same month, his campaign to purge the Maroons intensified. Some of the courts martial were illegally constituted - as Lord Bathurst, Secretary of State for War and the Colonies, later pointed out - but Ainslie appeared uninterested in due process.

The court martial was a military court, but, ironically, it was composed of civilian members of the local Militia drawn from the parishes. Militia members were not required to be trained in legal affairs but the Judge Advocate sat with them to advise on points of law. Those who featured as both judge and jury in the courts martial were in most cases planters and government officials; they were, as Lord Bathurst commented, not without their prejudices. The defendants had no legal representation and there was no jury.

The courts martial were held in the Market House on Roseau's bay front, adjoining the market place (now known as the Old Market), rather than the Court House which had been destroyed in the hurricanes of the previous year. The Market House, built four years earlier in 1810, was the administrative centre for the activities of the market place where executions and slave auctions took place. Until recently, it housed the Dominica Museum.

Ainslie's most effective weapon in his war against the Maroons was the newly formed Loyal Dominica Rangers, who consisted of "trusty" slaves, recruited through their owners. Paid, fed, armed and provided with uniforms, they were promised their freedom if they captured or killed a Maroon chief. The Rangers knew the forests and proved skilled in guerrilla warfare.

These trials of Maroons and their enslaved allies (four of the executed were not runaways but were charged with "harbouring and supplying runaways") provide detailed information about both Maroon and plantation society. They are the raw material from which a much fuller picture of resistance and of life among the Neg Mawon might one day be conjured.

16 JANUARY 1814

Ainslie declared martial law on this day. In this letter to Bathurst, he defended this policy and his plan for raising a separate corps of Black troops - the Loyal Dominica Rangers - to pursue the Maroons.

> I do myself the honour to acquaint your Lordship that I have judged proper to put this colony under martial law for one month from the 16th Instant. The runaway slaves who have been for 30 years established in the almost inaccessible mountains of Dominica, having become very troublesome from the depredations they were committing. I adopted this measure at the same time that I sent out parties from the Militia aided by a small force of Black troops. Some camps have been destroyed, a good number of the runaways have returned to their masters and I have little doubt, that at the expiration of the existence of martial law when, a colonial corps of Rangers now in training is to be posted to the principal camp, the colony will be comparatively freed from this evil. (CO 71/49)

Dominica's Militia was distinct from the troops of the British army stationed in Dominica. Under the Militia Act, all free men between 16 and 50 had to serve in the Militia of their parish. The Militia operated as a kind of Home Guard to defend the rest of the population against slave uprisings. William Bremner did not hold the Militia in high regard. Here, he explains its limitations.

> The Militia consisting chiefly of the managers and overseers of the plantations could be ill-spared for the superintendence of those concerns [on the estates], which suffered by their absence... Nor were they the sort of force likely to be able long to cope with such enemies, their habits and modes of life not being such as to render it probable they could long endure the excessive fatigue, numerous privations and constant exposure to the weather necessarily attending a service of this nature. (WB, p150)

In contrast, the Corps or Loyal Dominica Rangers served Ainslie's needs well. Bremner described how the Rangers were led by Captain Savarin, a former army lieutenant, assisted by Sergeant Nash, a free black man who had performed a similar role in St Vincent.

[The Ranger Corps] was to embody a number of faithful slaves, and to put arms into their hands under proper officers. About 60 of these were speedily enrolled, accoutred, and clothed in an appropriate manner*: and rations and provisions were issued to them from the Government stores. The principal difficulty was to find a commander capable of the arduous task... All eyes were therefore turned to Mr Savarin who had several years before been employed with much success in a similar way, when a lieutenant in the army, but as he had quitted the service and had now a wife and a large family, and a property of his own to superintend, was doubtful whether he would now venture to undertake so laborious an occupation. He was however prevailed on by the Governor to accept the commission... he was most ably seconded in his exertions to train his recruits to the business, by a free Negro man named Nash, who was appointed Sergeant Major of the Corps, and who had lately arrived from St Vincent, in which colony he had been of essential use in a similar office... (*at the expense of the colony, who also undertook to pay the owners a stipulated hire per day, and rations etc) (WB, p152)

THE COURTS MARTIAL

15 January to 22 May 1814

With the declaration of martial law in Dominica, cases were heard by courts martial and not by the courts of special sessions. The courts martial, which sat on 11 occasions between January 15 and May 22 1814, heard the cases of 44 defendants. Twelve people were sentenced to death during the courts martial; 10 were executed in a period of four months (from January to May 1814). Five of the condemned were women: three were hanged, one called Rebecca was pardoned "at the gallows" and one, Hester, who was pregnant, died in jail. Two male defendants were found not guilty, two women discharged through ill-health and three women, including Rebecca, were pardoned.

Beyond the basic, documented facts surrounding each case, how accurate are the accounts of these courts martial? It is difficult to know. However, there is a clue in this letter from Benjamin Lucas, Commander in Chief of the colony after Governor Ainslie's departure from Dominica, to Bathurst.

> I have also been unable to get the minutes of the courts martial on the trials of runaway slaves copied to go by this packet. The Judge Advocate [WW Glanville] (who embarked for England last month) having written them in so careless a manner and on separate sheets of paper with contractions, erasures and interlineations, that the clerk I employed for the occasion can with difficulty read them. These, however, and the minutes of the special sessions, I shall also have the honour to transmit by the next packet. (CO 71/50)

In addition to Lucas' claims that the minutes had been carelessly written, one might also speculate whether some evidence was omitted, either intentionally or by mistake. Adding to these ambiguities is the fact that some of the evidence is in reported speech rather than direct speech, thus rendering it less immediate and possibly less accurate.

However compromised, the evidence, especially that in direct speech, is revealing. It is unusual - in the history of slavery in the Caribbean - to hear the voices of the enslaved. Despite official apathy, antipathy, inefficiency, bureaucracy, inertia and so on, these voices survive, and we hear their words as defendants, as witnesses and as the members of the Loyal Dominica Rangers.

However we interpret this material, these accounts further our understanding of the relationships between the enslaved and the Maroons - a key factor in strengthening the power of the Maroons - and of plantation society itself. The Maroons obtained goods (salt, guns, tobacco, smoked fish and so on) and services (information) from the enslaved. This complex network in itself undermined the institution of slavery.

As the evidence shows, a cast of witnesses - owners, managers, overseers, Rangers, soldiers, slaves and captured Maroons - were brought to testify. Sometimes the defendant cross-examined the witnesses or was asked if he or she had anything to say.

In the end, justice was summary: without representation, the balance of power was stacked against the defendants, and punishment - flogging, banishment, working in chains, and execution - was brutal. As William Bremner commented in his memoirs, the hanging and disposal of the hanged body in public view aimed to terrorise by example. In some instances, the head of the executed man or woman was displayed on a pole in the market place or returned to the estate, also for exhibition, while the body was hung in chains or burned by the sea shore.

The first court martial sat on the weekend of 15 and 16 January.[1] *The Judge Advocate was the careless scribe, WW Glanville.*

Saturday and Sunday 15 and 16 JANUARY 1814
The TRIAL of JEAN PIERRE

Minutes of a court martial held at the Market House during martial law this 15 January 1814 by virtue of an order from Major General Ainslie for the trials of such prisoners as may be brought before them. Captain William Robinson, St Paul; Lieutenants Dowdy, Robinson, Matthews; Ensign Gloster. Judge Advocate, WW Glanville.

JEAN PIERRE, a Negro man belonging to Mr Grano, a runaway being brought before the court was accused by Lieut Stronach of the St Patrick Company of attempting to return [to] the runaways having a parcel of provision for the purpose of being carried up to the camp. Mr Stronach deposed that the prisoner was discovered coming from one of the estates in Grand Bay with a large bundle of wahwahs or wild yams. He was taken by the sentry and confessed he had been away for two months and that his wife and child had been taken the same morning by a private party from Mr Hiriart. He was going up to the camp.

COURT: Where did you take him?
STRONACH: I took him in Pichelin on the public road, he was just going to cut into the woods when the sentry stopped him.
COURT: When the sentry presented his piece to him to fire, he said in French, "I am coming." Did he appear to avoid the sentry?
STRONACH: He did.
COURT: Mr Grano says the Negro belongs to him. He has been absent since November last and has been twice runaway.
Mr Stronach further deposed, he [Jean Pierre] said he was chased by the

party who took his wife but he was too swift for them and he returned to his old position.

The prisoner being asked what he had to say for himself answered nothing.

[The trial of Jean Pierre was then adjourned and resumed the next day.]

The next defendant was Peter, a fisherman from Hillsborough estate at the mouth of the Layou River, about eight miles from Roseau. The trial of Peter and that of six others from Hillsborough (see page 51) provides some of the most extensive information of all the courts martial about life on the estates and the different forms of resistance; importantly, the evidence also reveals that enslaved people had a sense of their rights. This trial shows that white violence was ubiquitous, both in everyday life on the plantations and as a tool of the state. However it also suggests that slaves negotiated a sort of settlement with the slave system, within whose parameters they could somehow exist. In this instance, it was when this arrangement broke down - when conditions were no longer tenable - that the enslaved rebelled as did these Hillsborough "activists".

The Hillsborough estate at this time was run by a manager assisted by other white men employed as overseers or clerks, while William Bremner was the estate attorney. The absentee landlady was Catherine Greg, who lived in a London suburb. Her late husband, John Greg, had been the colonial surveyor of Dominica and had settled Hillsborough in 1765. At Catherine Greg's death in 1820, the estate passed to Greg's nephews, one of whom, Samuel Greg, became a pioneer of the English industrial revolution developing a cotton mill at Quarry Bank, outside Manchester. By the 1830s it had become the largest of its kind in England. It is now a National Trust property.

As Hillsborough's attorney, Bremner was closely involved in the events at Hillsborough that January and his memoirs provide some illuminating details. Some of his narrative is, unsurprisingly, at variance with the evidence of the Hillsborough enslaved on trial but Bremner's account is much fuller than that of the minutes of the trial, and it gives us the background.

Bremner wrote that a slave named Frank had died during the night from what others described as a flogging by the manager. The next day, 20 slaves left the estate to walk to Roseau to see Governor Ainslie and demand that the Hillsborough manager be sacked. Ainslie told them to go back to work. In response, they went into the woods. Peter, described by Bremner as "one of the most shrewd slaves on the estate", was told to take some Rangers to find them. Bremner suggests that Peter well knew where they were but deliberately misled the Rangers. In refusing Bremner's promise of money in return for tracking down the runaways, Peter's response, said Bremner, was a "contemptuous sneer".

This is Bremner's version of events:

> At this period (on the 5th Jan, 1814) a circumstance occurred on a plantation under my charge, which placed this matter in a pretty strong point of view. A body of 20 Negroes belonging to Hillsboro' estate, came up to town to complain to the Governor that the manager, Mr Venn[2], had murdered a Negro there by flogging him to death. His Excellency immediately sent for me and communicated this information. I said, Mr B's [V?] character was such that I could scarcely credit his being capable of such an act, but that the best method of ascertaining the truth would be for the coroner to hold an inquest on the body. This was done immediately and the verdict was that the man had died by the visitation of God, for there was not the smallest mark of violence. And it turned out that the Negro had gone to the hospital the day before with what appeared to the manager a trifling illness, for which he gave him a dose of salts, and that

he was much astonished and deeply grieved to find him dead next morning. But he declared most solemnly (and I sincerely believed him) that he never once laid his hand on the man.

In the meantime I remonstrated with the Negroes in town on the impropriety of such a body of them leaving the estate at once, observing that it would have been sufficient if one had come to give the information, but that they might rest assured, if there were any grounds for their accusation, the manager should not go unpunished. I then apprised them of the mode the Governor had directed to enquire into the fact, and recommended it to them to return quietly to the plantation, informing them at the same time I would myself visit the estate as soon as possible, in order to investigate the matter further. The same evening Mr V came to town, evidently much distressed with what had occurred, but complained

Left: the Greg family, owners of Hillsborough estate where one of the most important Maroon revolts took place, in 1814. Samuel Greg (fourth right) became a cotton king in England. Below: the overseers' houses and works at Hillsborough. Right: "Your time is done now", the words of Peter, the enslaved fisherman of Hillsborough, from his court martial in January 1814. He was hanged.

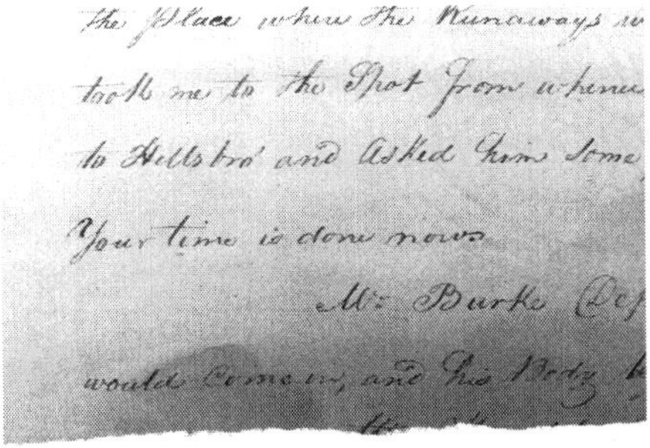
the place where the Runaways w
took me to the Spot from whence
to Hillsbro' and Asked him some
Your time is done now
Mr Burke Dep
would come in, and his Body b

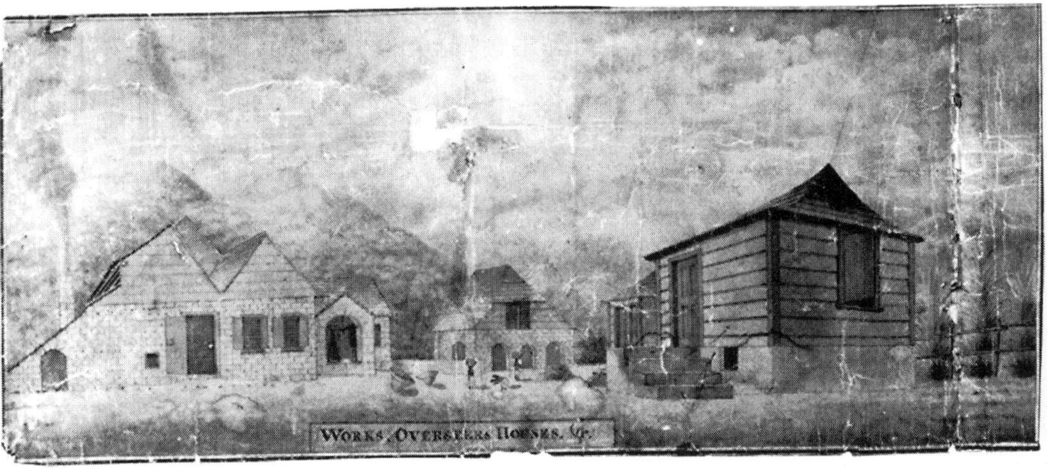

greatly of the complete insubordination of the gang since the beginning of the year, and said if something was not done to reduce them to discipline his authority was at an end, and that it would be better for him to quit the estate.

I therefore determined to visit the property next morning, expecting to find the Negroes returned to their duty. But when I arrived there nothing had been heard of them. Persuaded as I was that they were at no great distance, and that some of those on the estate were acquainted with their lurking place, I called the driver and some of the other confidential people, and advised them to inform the gang generally that they had better endeavour to bring in their friends quietly, and not drive me to harsh measures. (WB, pp144-46)

Bremner professed that he was willing to deal leniently with the Hillsborough enslaved if they acknowledged a ringleader. Instead they expressed solidarity, saying "with great clamour" that "if I punished one I must punish all". Bremner identified a woman called Sarah as being "at the bottom of the plot".

About 7 in the evening, it being now dark, they all made their appearance. After remonstrating with them on the enormity of bringing so infamous a false charge against Mr V and with absenting themselves from their duty without any cause of complaint, I said I was disposed, however, to deal mildly with them, and that if they would give me up their ringleader, I would pardon the rest. Instead of doing so, however, they renewed their accusations against Mr V and said with great clamour, if I punished one I must punish all. To this I replied that in such a case I must follow my own judgment who was the principal delinquent, and immediately laid hold of a woman named Sarah, whom I had some reasons to believe to be at the bottom of the plot. Upon this all the rest instantly ran off, and dispersed among the cane pieces, under cover of the darkness. In a moment all was dead silence, nor could one of the delinquents be found that night. Unavoidable business compelled me to return to Roseau immediately, but I left orders with the white people on the estate to keep a strict watch during the night, and directed Mr V to write me early in the morning.

Next day there was no appearance of their return; on the contrary two more had absented.

Convinced that gentle means were not now likely to succeed, I applied to the Governor for a military force! The guide, whom I selected to conduct this party to the spot, where the runaways were hid, was a Negro named Peter, one of the most shrewd slaves on the estate, whose wife was one of the absentees, and who I was therefore certain must know of their place of concealment. This man had some years before been capitally tried for setting fire to the mogass houses (a very important part of the sugar works, where the fuel is kept), which were burnt down to the ground with all their contents, and threatened the destruction of the whole plantation. On that occasion he was acquitted for want of evidence, but he afterwards acknowledged his guilt and was pardoned as a very useful man on the property. I told him he had now an excellent opportunity of retrieving his character, and of rendering his owner essential service; and I held out to him two heavy Joanneses[3], which I assured him he should receive as a reward the moment he returned from showing the soldiers to the place where the runaways were hid. He affected great willingness and the party set off.

After leading them a long way round about, he said they were at last arrived at the spot. But when they got there no living being was to be found. He now pretended the runaways must have decamped a short time before, but that he had a pretty good notion of the place of their retreat, pointing to a distant ridge, to gain which, however, they must return to the plantation. Although suspicion began already to be entertained that he was misleading the detachment, it was determined to make another attempt. After they had rested sufficiently, I desired he would prepare to get off again. To this he replied it was of no use to go till a particular time he named, and that he would not go till then. Confirmed in my suspicions by this refusal, and by his general mysterious conduct (which seemed calculated to afford time to the runaways to learn our proceedings) I told him shortly, his fate depended on the part he was now to act, and that reward or punishment lay within his reach. To this caution he returned no other answer but a contemptuous sneer.

The party, however, went off again with Peter in custody, but after scrambling for part of two days over hills and dales, crags and precipices, there seemed no likelihood of his leading them to the desired spot. The commander of the military detachment remonstrated and threatened but in vain. At last, indeed, the fellow had the assurance to declare that, although he knew very well where the Negroes were, he would not tell, till Mr V was discharged from the estate. The party were therefore finally obliged to return to H [Hillsborough] without being able to see any of the runaways. I was now indeed exceedingly perplexed how to proceed, but at last I determined to keep a strict watch on Peter, who I was thoroughly satisfied was concerned in this conspiracy. I therefore ordered him to be sent to the gaol of Roseau, to abide the issue of the business.

... A few days after Peter was sent into confinement, one of the runaways from H named Candau, voluntarily returned to the estate. This woman, on being strictly interrogated, confessed that Peter had been the instigator of the plot there, and that he had held communication with the Negroes who had run away from the estate, and had supplied them with provisions during their absence. I now resolved to bring this offender to trial and therefore reported the case to the Governor, who ordered a court martial to assemble for that purpose. The charges being clearly proved, he was condemned to be hanged, his head stuck up upon a pole in the market place of Roseau, and his body hung in chains on the most conspicuous part of the plantation to which he belonged. All this sentence was duly carried into execution, and the very same day the whole of the absentees from H returned to their duty. This same Peter acknowledged just before his execution that he had administered poison to the former manager, Mr Blackman, which had proved the cause of his death, and said he died an example to the rest of the gang. (WB, pp146-51)

The evidence for Peter's trial is not as full as Dr Bremner's account. The first part relied on the evidence of Mr Venn (of Hillsborough estate) who painted a picture of Peter as defiant: when asked questions all he would say was "Your time is done now".

PETER, belonging to Hillsborough was charged by Doctor Bremner of exciting a mutiny amongst 20 of the Negroes upon the estate furnishing them with provision and other supplies while runaway.

Mr Venn, being sworn, deposed that the prisoner he supposed was the man of the head of above 22 Negroes, his reason for supposing so was that this man, after the Negroes had made their complaint to the Governor, he was sent by the witness to tell the Negroes that he desired to see them. They answered they would not see him neither would they return as long as he was on the estate.

"I ordered him to go back and tell them that if they would neither see him or hear from him, Governor would send a party to bring in by force. His answer was that if Governor send a party after them, they would strive for their heads and leave their bodies in the woods. About 10 o'clock in the evening Dr Bremner arrived and said that a party was coming from Roseau and requested me to take out Peter as a guide. I sent for Peter but I could not find him. I was then obliged to go out with some others, Tommy and John Louis. After we had been out for some time we arrived at two watch houses about two miles from the camp where I supposed they were. I took one party of four men and John Louis took another party of four men.

"In the watch house I examined, I found nothing, but in the one examined by John Louis he found Peter with a large stick and cutlass and three other Negroes who made their escape. Peter then came down and joined the whole party. I asked if he would show me the place where the runaways were. He said yes he would show me where they had been. He took me to the spot from whence the Negroes had been gone about six hours. I returned to Hillsbro and asked him some further questions to which he gave no other answer than 'Your time is done now'."

Mr Burke deposed that the prisoner said this time nothing but his head would come in and his body left in the woods.

Mr Wright deposed he had the charge of a party of soldiers on Sunday night. "I questioned the prisoner with respect of his being able to show me the camp and from his discourse with me he appeared to be able to show me the camp. He said he did but we went and finding he deceived me I put him in confinement."

Bandis belonging to Hillsbro deposed that she was one of those who came to complain to the Governor. The Governor said you must go home to the plantation. She answered, "We are all afraid to go upon the plantation lest the manager should flog us," and she went into the woods. When they went up to the woods they sat down and she saw a Negro coming from Tarow who asked them if they were there.

Nicky, a Negro belonging to the estate, divided the Negroes into two parts and gave some instruction. While they were out, Peter brought them some yams about half a bag 24 [?] and told them they would be damned fools to come back to the estate. He only said so once. (CO 71/51)

At this juncture, Peter's trial was adjourned and Jean Pierre's trial continued.

The prisoner Jean Pierre being asked what he had to say why sentence of death should not be passed upon. He said he was coming to surrender but three Negroes of Mr Hiriart named Matadore, Despesse and Pierre prevented him. He asked Matadore if he was safe where he was. He answered, "Yes", for the detachment was going to windward.

The court being cleared proceeded to take in consideration the charge against the prisoner Jean Pierre and are of opinion that the same is proved and ***do sentence him to be hanged*** at such time and place as the Governor shall appoint.

MR ROBINSON, CAPTAIN AND PRESIDENT.

Approved [by] *GEO ROBT AINSLIE* (CO 71/51)

When Peter's trial resumed on 16 January, the court was told that Peter had agreed to help the soldiers find the Hillsborough "runaways". Peter's words would suggest he felt in control of the situation - he knew the terrain, his skills were recognised, he made demands and he hoped to be rewarded. While he was found guilty, the court asked that his life be spared. Was he too useful a man to lose? Whatever the case, Ainslie decided that Peter should be executed.

The court having met pursuant to adjournment and proceeded with the trial of Peter, Sergeant Wm Rowan of the 4th West Indian regiment, being sworn, deposed. On Saturday the 8th inst, he was sent down by Major Jack with a party of six men. They arrived at Layou. Peter was apprehended by him in a watch house. He asked Peter if he could show him where the Negroes were. Peter said yes. They went with Peter until they slept. One night, in a camp, Peter said he would show him no other camp until the manager was removed from the plantation; as long as the manager remained the Negroes would not come in. Peter told him to take the manager to town and he would bring in all the Negroes. When he found Peter would not proceed, he returned to town.

Peter being asked if he had any questions to ask of the witness said he had none. The proceedings being closed, the prisoner was called upon to know what he had to say for himself. He said he did not runaway, the manager sent him out to tell the Negroes to come back to their service. He is always in the habit of bringing in the runaways from the estate.

"When I go out I always have victuals in my pocket and when I meet them I makes them food and catch them and bring them home to the manager. I left the runaways telling them the manager said they must come home. They said they would not until the manager left the estate. I reckoned how many there were and came and told the manager. He told me I must stop and he would send for the hunter (meaning the Sergeant and his party). After the hunter came I took the hunter to the places where I left them; after I came there they were already gone. He asked me if I did not know of any other place. I said I know the Big Camp but we have not men enough to go there. The last words I said were, 'Please God we go after them with plenty of troops we will make a good haul, and if the Governor is pleased with me I hope he will take me from the estate'."

Thomas Henderson Esquire, who lived as manager of the estate was called upon to give the court for a character of the prisoner. Being sworn he deposed that the prisoner has been employed as a fisherman, he has sent him after the skulkers and sometimes he has brought them in. He believes that the prisoner had great influence with the gang and he has no doubt of his communicating with them as he is well acquainted with the woods.

COURT: Was he in the habit of staying out after the runaways two or three days?
HENDERSON: Yes, sometimes for a week.

The court being cleared proceeded to take in consideration the charge against the prisoner and the evidence in support of it and having duly considered the same are of the opinion that he is guilty of the charge brought against him, and do therefore sentence him ***to be hanged at such time and place as the Governor shall appoint***. But the court finding him that he is a fit and proper person to act as a guide to the camps in the Layou and he, having professed a willingness to act as such, recommend to the Governor to employ him in that capacity provided he shall faithfully act as such and that he be afterwards banished the island for life.
WW GLANVILLE, JUDGE ADVOCATE
WM ROBINSON, CAPTAIN AND PRESIDENT

I approve and order the sentence to be carried with effect tomorrow at the usual hour, the head to be cut off and put on a pike in the market place, the body to be hung in chains on Hillsborough estate.
GEORGE R AINSLIE (CO 71/51)

The TRIAL of HECTOR

Hector was charged with being a runaway, found guilty and sentenced to flogging, one of the most common punishments given by the slave courts of the time in Dominica. It was usual in the British West Indies to limit floggings to 39 lashes[4] (according to Biblical tradition, 40 lashes would kill a man) and Dominican law was no exception. Yet both the courts martial and those of special sessions sentenced men to 100 lashes (the maximum for women was 50). In Hector's trial, the minutes are confusing. A sentence of 100 lashes was initially remitted; but the minutes then suggest that Ainslie changed an original sentence of 39 lashes to 100 lashes.

The court being opened proceeded with the trial of a Negro named **HECTOR** taken by Mr Elisonde and accused of being a runaway.

Mr Lionne deposed the prisoner has been absent about 15 days and was taken in his own estate about the 7th instant. Being asked if he often runaway he says when he has to go to Point Michel he hides himself.

Mr Elisonde, being sworn, that he took him about three o'clock in the morning on Mr Lionne's coffee estate with the party. He was returning home, he had a middling bundle of wahwahs. He told the witness he had an ajoupa in the woods near Mr Lionne's estate and that he been absent about a fortnight or three weeks. He told the witness the reason for running away was that he did not get his allowance of clothes and provisions and the witness declared that the prisoner was almost naked when taken.

The prisoner being asked what he had to say in his defence, said a mulatto, belonging to his master named George, induced him to run away by telling him his master was not good.

The court being cleared adjudged the prisoner to receive 100 lashes in the market place and be worked in the galley gang for six months.

WW GLANVILLE, JUDGE ADVOCATE

WM ROBINSON, CAPTAIN AND PRESIDENT

Approved *GEO R AINSLIE, GOVERNOR*. Lashes remitted. (CO 71/51)

The TRIAL of RACHEL

The next case was of Rachel, the first woman to be brought before the court. She was the wife of Jean Pierre, and was also from Mr Grano's estate. She was described by her owner as being of "good character" who was enticed away by her husband, who had been sentenced to death earlier.

RACHEL, a Negro woman, belonging to Mr Grano, taken up by a detachment of Mr Hiriart's Negroes, a runaway, was brought before the court.

Cupid, a Negro belonging to Mr Hiriart, being sworn, deposed that he was sent into the woods in order after the runaways. Just before daylight he went up to an ajoupa and found this woman and two children. The woman attempted to escape, they fired a musket after her, she stopped as soon as they fired. They took what belonged to her and set fire to the hut. They took her to Mr Hiriart's estate and put her in irons. The hut was at a considerable distance in the woods upon the top of a high ridge.

COURT: What did the prisoner do when you took her?
CUPID: She began to cry.

The prisoner being asked if she had any questions to put to the witness answered she had none.
Thimoth [witness]. That he belonged to the same party as Cupid. She was taken far in the woods.

The prisoner being called upon for her defence said that Matadore came once to her hut and eats there and that he brought her a bottle of salt.
Mr Grano deposed that she belongs to him and is a very good woman, that she never absented herself before and believes she was enticed there by her husband Jean Pierre. He has owned [her] for about 12 years.

The court being cleared were of opinion that the prisoner receive 50 lashes in the public market and be worked for three months in the galley gang. The court have been lenient in this sentence in consequence of her good character given her by her master and from every probability that she was induced by the artifices of her husband.[5]

The court having reason to believe that Matadore, a Negro belonging to Mr Hiriart, appears to be in some degree implicated, ordered him to be sent to jail to be brought up at the sitting of the next court martial. [No further mention was made of Matadore.]
WM ROBINSON, CAPTAIN AND PRESIDENT
Approved *GEO R AINSLIE, GOVERNOR*. Lashes remitted.

The President having waited upon the Governor with the minutes of the court martial, His Excellency recommended to the court to reconsider the sentence passed upon Hector taking into consideration the peculiar circumstances of the country.

The court was cleared and proceeded to reconsider the sentence passed upon Hector and taking into deliberation the circumstances of the colony, the daily outrages of the runaways and the necessity of making examples of such prisoners as may be found guilty do sentence him to receive one hundred lashes instead of 39 as before adjudged to be inflicted upon him. (CO 71/51)

The TRIALS of DICK, SARAH, HETTY, PENNY, PLACET and DANIEL

The following trial was closely linked to that of Peter from Hillsborough. The six enslaved tried here were also from Hillsborough and were accused of being the leaders of the group who protested about the death of Frank. One of them was called Sarah, whom Bremner described as "the ringleader" and who appeared to have played a key role in initiating the meeting with Governor Ainslie. In the evidence, the defendants explained their reason for leaving the estate echoing Bremner's account. Sarah was, like the others, convicted, and was given a sentence of 50 lashes but unlike the others she was reprieved.

DICK (SARAH, HETTY, PENNY and **PLACET)**, a Negro belonging to Hillsbro, charged with having been one of 20 Negroes who absented themselves from their duty on Wednesday the 5 January inst. Mr Venn deposed that he [Dick] absented himself from his duty with about 20 more on the 5 January inst and had been away for upwards of a fortnight, that Dick came in yesterday morning, that all the prisoners are equally guilty, that all but Dick and **DANIEL** [also charged but not originally named] came in on Wednesday morning.

COURT: Do you know the reason of their quitting the estate?
MR VENN: From a Negro named Frank dying suddenly in the sick house. They supposed he must have been either poisoned or whipped to death by him.

COURT: Was any of the prisoners more active than the others in exciting them to go away?
MR VENN: I do not know.
MR FOURNIER [witness] that in the morning of the 5 instant, John came and brought the news that Frank was dead, and the first person who spoke in the field was Sarah. She said, "Well you see that." I said to them, "I see very [missing word] you won't work none," and everyone was quiet until the bell rang for breakfast. When I came back I found almost all the Negroes gone. I called the driver, and asked where the people were. He said they are gone to their Negro houses for their breakfast. I sent the driver to the Negro houses where he stopped a short time and went up myself. When I was on the road to go to the Negro houses I heard the people had gone to Roseau. I came to Mr Venn's house and I found him writing and the driver there.
COURT: Have any of those people come to their work since the 5th January? [No record is given of the answer to this question.]

The prisoners being asked if they had anything to say, Dick said he returned to the estate but he did not go to work. The reason he left the estate was on account of the death of Frank. That Frank complained of being sick and the manager would not pay any attention to him and made him go to the field and flogged him, and the Negro Frank died the day after in the sick house, that he was only absent with his brother Daniel. The others said they had nothing to say.

Daniel, Mr Venn deposed, he had been absent since the 7th January and came in yesterday morning that he is equally guilty with the rest. The prisoner said he got frightened and went away.

The court being cleared were of opinion that the prisoners were guilty and adjudge the men Dick and Daniel to receive 100 lashes each in the market place and the woman Sarah 50 and the other prisoners 50 each.
WW GLANVILLE, JUDGE ADVOCATE
THOMAS HAYES, CAPTAIN AND PRESIDENT

I approve and order the sentence to be carried into execution tomorrow

between the hours of ten and twelve.
GEO R AINSLIE, GOVERNOR AND MAJOR GENERAL (CO 71/51)

28 JANUARY 1814
The TRIAL of JOSEPH

The following week there was another court martial. The trial documents do not show who sat at this trial. They do, however, show the direct words of the witnesses in some detail and mention the chief, Elephant, and his camp in the south of the island. Joseph was found "not guilty".

JOSEPH, belonging to Mr Dubocq, charged with supplying the runaways with salt and other provisions.

Paul [witness], belonging to Nelson's Rest, being sworn in.
COURT: Do he know the prisoner?
PAUL: Yes, I do. I knew him in the camp when he was a runaway.
COURT: Were you both in the same camp?
PAUL: No we were not. I saw him once and Joseph went away.
COURT: When did you see him?
PAUL: The first time I went to the camp I saw Joseph.
COURT: What camp was it?
PAUL: In Elephant's camp
COURT: Where [sic] camp is it?
PAUL: The same Mr Hiriat attacked and burnt.
COURT: Do you know that Joseph brought provisions to the camp at any time you were there?
PAUL: I do not know. The first day I went to the camp, it was the first day Joseph surrendered to his master.
COURT: Did you see him bring salt?
PAUL: No I never did.

Marie Claire [witness]
COURT: Do you know the prisoner?
MARIE CLAIRE: Yes

COURT: When was the first time and where?
MARIE CLAIRE: When I runaway I found Joseph in the camp.
COURT: In what camp?
MARIE CLAIRE: In Debouche's camp
COURT: In what camp were you when Paul joined you?
MARIE CLAIRE: In Elephant's camp. We were three days in Debouche's camp and from thence they went to Elephant's and Joseph said, "Take good cheer I am going to surrender."
COURT: Did you ever see Joseph come to the camp after he surrendered?
MARIE CLAIRE: No I never did
COURT: Did you ever know that Joseph sent salt to the camps?
She says that Elephant and Gomier said that Joseph supplied them.
COURT: Did he bring salt?
MARIE CLAIRE: No I never saw him. I only heard it from Elephant and Gomier.

The court being cleared and having taken the charge into consideration and the evidence are of opinion that he is not guilty.
WW GLANVILLE, JUDGE ADVOCATE
THOMAS HAYES, CAPTAIN AND PRESIDENT (CO 71/51)

The TRIAL of PIERRE

In the next case, the defendant Pierre, of Mt Eolus estate near Portsmouth in the north of the island, cross-examined two witnesses. Pierre, like Peter, had been asked to go in search of "runaways" and bring them back to the estate. When Pierre questioned the witnesses he appeared to be trying to establish that he had asked them to return and had told them that they would not be punished if they did so.

PIERRE, belonging to Mt Eolus estate, charged with encouraging the Negroes upon that estate who had absented themselves to stay away from their duty.

[Unnamed witness]
On the 7th November, ten of Mount Eolus Negroes who had absented

themselves from their duty on the 21st came in on the 25th. I sent the prisoner to come to their owner's duty and I would forgive them. He returned saying they would not come in and I asked him for what reason. He looked round, shook his head and said they were afraid of being punished. In the afternoon I got five free people of colour to go in pursuit of them with this man Pierre as a guide. The people returned in the evening saying they found one dead, on the 24th. I got Mr Middleton, Mr Casey and Mr O'Brien as neighbours to go and look at the body. On the 1 December, this man absented himself, on the 15th day the other eight surrendered explaining that Pierre frightened them away. I asked them how Pierre could frighten them away. They first said he eat wahwah with them, and told them to take their things and go further away as I was getting free people to go after them.

Pierre was brought home on the 12 January by a Negro of Mr Kyries and I paid a Joe for having him caught.

ALPHONSE [witness]
COURT: When Pierre came to bring you home what did he say?
ALPHONSE: When Pierre came to the watch house where they were, he told them the manager sent him to bring them home, and if they would not come they might stay if they liked. Pierre told them the manager was going to get free people to take them and they must go further off.
COURT: Did you go away in consequence of what Pierre said?
ALPHONSE: Yes.
COURT: What did you say when Pierre told you come in?
ALPHONSE: I said maybe master will flog me.
COURT: What did Pierre say?
ALPHONSE: He said you must [go] further and not stay in the same place.
COURT: Did Pierre tell you your master would flog you?
ALPHONSE: Yes.
COURT: Did Pierre try to bring you back?
ALPHONSE: No, he did not want us to come back.
COURT: Suppose Pierre had told you to come in would you come in?
ALPHONSE: Yes.

COURT: Where did you get victuals?
ALPHONSE: From our grounds.
COURT: Did Pierre give you any?
[no answer recorded]
COURT: When Pierre ran away did he come?
ALPHONSE: No we never saw him.

[Pierre cross-examines Alphonse]
PIERRE: Did I not tell you the manager desired you to come to your work?
ALPHONSE: Yes you did.
PIERRE: What answer did you make? Did you not say there was no use of going back and you would get punished?
ALPHONSE: No. Pierre asked him for something to eat.
PIERRE: Did I not say the manager would not punish you?
ALPHONSE: No.

Marie-Francoise [witness]
The day the manager sent him he came to us - we run when we saw him; we afterwards went to him. He told us the manager said we must come home. He then said he felt peckish. We gave him some yam. He roasted and eat it. He then said if it was he, he would never come home that the manager would punish them. I made answer it is very hard the manager should send for us to punish us. I went where the stock [missing word?] – at first we went in a pasture. He told us to go further and we did so.

[Pierre cross-examines Marie-Francoise]
PIERRE: When I went to you did I not tell you the manager sent me for you and he would not punish you.
MARIE-FRANCOISE: Yes you said so.

The prisoner being asked for his defence said that the manager sent to them to tell them to come to their duty. She, the witness Marie-Francoise, said it was very hard to come down to be punished and she would have her head cut off before. I asked them the last word before I went and they said the same thing.

The court being cleared proceeded to take the charge against the prisoner into consideration and having considered the evidence in support of the same are of the opinion that he is guilty of the same and do sentence him to 100 lashes and to be worked for six months in the galley gang.
WW GLANVILLE, JUDGE ADVOCATE
THOMAS HAYES, CAPTAIN AND PRESIDENT

Approved to be carried into immediate execution by the Marshal for which this authority.
GEO R AINSLIE, GOVERNOR (CO 71/51)

The TRIAL of CHARLES

In this case, the defendant said that he ran away because of unreasonable demands made of him by his owner. Charles is the only defendant to mention Governor Ainslie's proclamations. He said that in the light of the proclamation he had wanted to surrender but Jacko, the chief of the camp, had stopped him and would have "cut him to pieces" if he had found him.

CHARLES, belonging to Mr Bourgeau, charged with having run away from his owner for near 17 months.

Mr Desriviere being sworn that the prisoner was upon the estate of Mr [?] Bourgeau, his sister, and she told him he was runaway.

COURT: Do you know him to be runaway?
MR DESRIVIERE: I am often in the field at my sister's estate and I know the prisoner to be a runaway.
COURT: Did you know him before he ran away?
MR DESRIVIERE: Yes I did.
COURT: When was the last time you saw him?
MR DESRIVIERE: Since he has run away I only saw him this morning.
COURT: Before he ran away were you in the habit of seeing him at work?
MR DESRIVIERE: Yes I was.
COURT: Since his runaway he has always been absent from the estate

till this morning?

MR DESRIVIERE: Yes.

COURT: When you saw him this morning did he appear to come into surrender?

MR DESRIVIERE: No, he came with my drivers.

COURT: What account did he give of himself?

MR DESRIVIERE: He said he came to him and since he did not wish to stop on Mr Bourgeau's estate but he wished to be with him.

The prisoner had no questions to ask. The prisoner was asked what he had to say for himself. [He] said that his mistress sent him for two bundles of wood upon another estate. "I said to her, 'Mistress how can I bring two bundles of woods and the sun has set and I am sick.' She answered, 'She did not care.' I brought one bundle and left the others it being 8 o'clock at night. I went back the next day at 12 o'clock to split the others and my mistress asked me where was my grass. I brought the grass at night, and just as I brought the grass my mistress endeavoured to lay hold me and I made my escape. She said if you were to bring my father to ask forgiveness I would not pardon you, and that was the reason I ran away."

Since the proclamations of the Governor calling upon the Negroes to surrender, he was desirous of coming back but Jacko, the chief, told him he should not go. If he had attempted to escape he would kill him, and now that he has escaped if they had caught him they would cut him to pieces, that he went to dig wahwah and when he expressed a wish to come back they took from him what he had to dig wahwahs with.

The court being cleared proceeded to take into consideration the charges and are of opinion he is guilty thereof and so sentence him to receive in the public market place 100 lashes and to work in the galley gang for six months; the court has been so lenient in its sentence in consequence of the prisoner having returned to his owners.

WW GLANVILLE, JUDGE ADVOCATE

THOMAS HAYES, CAPTAIN AND PRESIDENT

I approve. *GEO R AINSLIE* (CO 71/51)

The TRIAL of AUGUSTIN

Mr Morau, the owner of the Negro, stating to the court that the Negro had been runaway about three months and had surrendered himself to his master but that he is an idiot and the court not deemed him a fit object for trial, ordered him to be discharged upon payment of fees.

7 FEBRUARY 1814

Chief Elephant, owned by George Anderson, was shot by the manager of Edenbro estate, according to the official lists of runaways sent to the Colonial Office in London.

Saturday 26 FEBRUARY 1814

The TRIAL of VICTOR

The records of Victor's trial are particularly illuminating about the exchange networks that existed between the enslaved and the Maroons. Victor was charged with supplying the Maroons with gunpowder, saltfish and tobacco; he was found guilty and hanged.

Proceedings of a court martial held by order of Major General Ainslie for the trial of all such prisoners as may be brought before them, Roseau 26 February. President, Major Constable, St George's Regiment; Captain Lowthwaite; Lieutenant Dodds, Lieutenant Court; Ensign Gloster, Judge Advocate, WW Glanville. The President and members being sworn and the Judge Advocate being sworn.

VICTOR, a Negro belonging to Pauline Giraudel, is charged with having supplied the runaways with gunpowder, saltfish and tobacco.

Sgt Noel L'Abbé of the St George's Regiment being duly sworn in deposed: "I went up with Captain Jacquin to go up to Pauline Giraudel's, the mistress of the prisoner, and [when] we appeared upon the estate we saw him and took him. I was ordered by the captain to tie him and to search his house and his mistress's house, and to take out what we found. There we found two fowling pieces in the mistress's house, and in the prisoner's a calabash of small shot, a camp kettle, a pail and an iron pot, a rush basket or haversack and one wahwah and nothing else."

The prisoner declined asking the witness any questions.

Papynard, belonging to the estate Mesdelices, being sworn deposed that he knows the prisoner, that he has been at his house twice with Sans Souci and Ignace, two runaways, that he was a runaway himself, that Victor was at home, that they went to get saltfish and tobacco, that Victor exchanged them for wahwahs, that Victor gave him the witness a moco[6] of salt and a moco tobacco and gave the other two bills worth of the same, that he gave them six bills worth of saltfish in the whole that he gave Victor three rush haversacks full of wahwah.

COURT: Did you ever come down with Elephant?

PAPYNARD: No, I never did. Elephant came down alone.

COURT: Did you ever get powder from Victor?

PAPYNARD: No but Sans Souci in my presence did, he bought a bottle.

COURT: Did Victor tell him where he got that powder?

PAPYNARD: No he did not.

COURT: Did you open the bottle?

PAPYNARD: Yes I did. I saw there was powder in it.

COURT: Do you know how much Sans Souci gave for the powder?

PAPYNARD: No I do not.

COURT: How many times did Victor give Sans Souci powder?

PAPYNARD: Three times.

COURT: Did he ever tell you when he got the powder?

PAPYNARD: No.

COURT: Do you know where he got the powder?

PAPYNARD: No. He never told us.

COURT: Did you ever or Sans Souci ask where he got the powder?

PAPYNARD: No I never did. If Sans Souci asked him, it was behind his [?] back.

COURT: Did he ever make any balls?

PAPYNARD: No he did not.

COURT: Where did you get the shot?

PAPYNARD: We melted down spoons for that purpose.
COURT: Did you or any of your companions borrow fowling pieces from Victor?
PAPYNARD: Yes. Sans Souci did.
COURT: Should you know it?
PAPYNARD: Yes.
COURT: Did he lend him [it] loaded?
PAPYNARD: No he did not.
COURT: Did they ever leave their guns at Victor's house?
PAPYNARD: Yes, when they came to town.
COURT: Have you been more than twice at Victor's house?
PAPYNARD: Twice only.
COURT: Did Victor ever come to the camp?
PAPYNARD: No, they always came to his house.
COURT: Is that the fowling piece?
PAPYNARD: No. It is Elephant's. I know it well. Elephant gave it to Victor to get his master named Vandrise to repair it. Elephant took off the lock and gave it to him.
COURT: Is this the same gun?
PAPYNARD: No, I am not acquainted with it.
COURT: Were you with them when they robbed and [illegible word] LaCorne's house?
PAPYNARD: No but Victor was.
COURT: How many were they when they went to LaCorne?
PAPYNARD: Six and this man.
COURT: Were you left in charge of Victor's house?
PAPYNARD: No they left me and one of his master's Negroes.
COURT: Is your master's Negro runaway?
PAPYNARD: No, he is no runaway.
COURT: Did you ever get powder or anything from Victor's master's Negro, Jean Louis?
PAPYNARD: No. I did not but Ignace got saltfish and salt. I only saw him get some once.

COURT: Has Jean Louis any muskets?

PAPYNARD: No he never [missing word] him or saw any.

COURT: When they went to LaCorne's, what did they take?

PAPYNARD: Seven rabbits, a quantity of clothes and two hogs.

COURT: Did Victor go to LaCorne's?

PAPYNARD: Yes, Victor brought up a bag of coffee.

COURT: When Victor went down had he a musket?

PAPYNARD: No, he had only a cutlass.

COURT: Did he carry down any powder or balls?

PAPYNARD: No, the others had guns but not Victor.

COURT: When they divided the booty what did Victor get?

PAPYNARD: Two quarters of a hog, a jacket and a shirt and two fowls.

COURT: Did Victor ever go on any robbing party?

PAPYNARD: Only twice to LaCorne's.

COURT: Did Victor share the booty?

PAPYNARD: Yes.

COURT: Was it divided at Victor's house?

PAPYNARD: No, on the road.

COURT: How long is it ago?

PAPYNARD: About a month ago.

COURT: What did he get the first time?

PAPYNARD: He did not get any clothes, only two fowls and one quarter of a hog.

COURT: Did Victor say that was his share of the booty?

PAPYNARD: Yes, both times.

COURT: Why did they not take you with them?

PAPYNARD: They were afraid he [?] would show the white people.

COURT: Do you know Victor's wife?

PAPYNARD: No, he has no wife at his house.

COURT: Did Jean Louis ever go down to rob?

PAPYNARD: No.

COURT: Did he ever get any share of the booty?

PAPYNARD: No, I do not know.

Victor cross-examines Papynard

VICTOR: Did you ever see me sell or give powder to Sans Souci?

PAPYNARD: Yes I did.

VICTOR: How many weeks is it ago?

PAPYNARD: Before Mr Ellison's party went out.

VICTOR: Did you see me with your own eyes go with the party to La Corne's?

PAPYNARD: Yes I was at your house. I saw you bring up the coffee.

VICTOR: How many times did you see me give powder to Sans Souci?

PAPYNARD: Twice.

VICTOR: Was it since the white people have been in the wood?

PAPYNARD: No before that.

VICTOR: How many times have you been to my house?

PAPYNARD: Twice.

VICTOR: Did your Master's Negro see me give him powder?

PAPYNARD: No he was not there; I saw you.

The court, being cleared to take into consideration the charge against the prisoner and the evidence in support, are of opinions that he is guilty of the same and ***do sentence him to be hanged*** at such time and place as the Governor shall appoint.

WW GLANVILLE, JUDGE ADVOCATE

DANIEL CONSTABLE, PRESIDENT

I approve and order the sentence to be carried into effect at the usual hour tomorrow being Sunday the 27th instant; after hanging till two hours the head to be stuck on a pole, the body again suspended by the arms till 5 o'clock when it must be burned on the beach.

GEO R AINSLIE GOVERNOR (CO 71/51)

2 MARCH 1814

Ainslie addressed the two legislative houses (the Council and the House of Assembly) and promised that the pursuit of the Maroons would continue so that "an evil of great and increasing magnitude" would be destroyed.

The operations carried on against the Maroons since martial law was proclaimed have been successful, 14 settlements burnt, the provision grounds (which at one place alone presented to the eye an extent of four miles of the finest plants) given up to public use, or entirely destroyed, the alternative alone remaining to the runaways of perishing from hunger in the woods or taking advantage of my proclamation to give themselves up. Already above 50 of these misguided wretches have returned to their masters and a considerable number have paid the forfeit of their lives, exclusive of those who have perished through want which must have been great when we reflect upon the large amount of men, women and children deprived of every means of subsistence except wild vegetables.

It is my intention not to relax in the least in pursuing the system of harassing the Maroons, and I hope, in very few weeks will accomplish our object, which circumstances not to be controlled by me, have hitherto prevented in the extirpation of an evil of great and increasing magnitude, and consequently security of property restored to the colonists.

I intend that the Ranger Corps shall remain permanently in the woods for the purpose of having parties on the alert in search of the fugitives. Twelve volunteers of people of colour have been added to that useful corps, who, I may [illegible word] promise will settle on allotments of Maroon lands, which I propose to give them, and thus open the communication between Layou and the Windward side of the island towards Pagua and Castle Bruce.[7]

Sunday 6 MARCH 1814
The TRIAL of JOE

Martial law had been extended until 1 March by order of a Council of War, but there are no records purporting to a Council of War being held after that date. The courts martial held after 1 March were, with one exception held on a Sunday, the day of the weekly market when Roseau would have been crowded with people, including the enslaved. It was also the day of execution - a fate that awaited Joe.

Proceedings of a court martial held by order of his Excellency Major General Ainslie for the trial of such prisoners as may be brought before them 6 March 1814. President, Major Constable, St George's Regiment; Captain Jacquin; Lieutenants Keay and Myler; Ensign Culpepper; Judge Advocate, WW Glanville.

JOE, a Negro belonging to the estate of Cubbin, was charged with harbouring and supplying the runaway slaves.

L. André Fournier Desmarinieres being sworn deposed that when the alarm was fired the runaways were sent after. He came from Cubbin's estate where he had been living at the time. The Negro Joe told him not to be afraid and not to go away because the runaways would not do him any harm, and if he did not trouble them and allowed them to pass he might stay in peace. He further deposed that he had communications with the runaways seeing him among them, that they passed sometimes in number of six, eight or 10 and Joe was with them at the times. There was a large piece of lead in the coffee house upon the estate. He asked to whom the lead [missing word]. Joe said it belonged to him. I asked him what he was going to do with it. He said he wanted it.

COURT: Do you know if he has ever supplied the runaways with provisions, salt, tobacco or any other article?
DESMARINIERES: No, not of my own knowledge.
COURT: Have you ever seen him in company with Elephant?
DESMARINIERES: Yes, often, five or six times.

The prisoner declined asking any questions.

Gervais, belonging to Mr Jacquin, being sworn that he knows the prisoner.
COURT: Did you ever see the runaways in his house?
GERVAIS: Yes, often.
COURT: Did you ever see Elephant in the prisoner's house?
GERVAIS: Yes, he was told he used go into the prisoner's house and Victor's,

that he heard Joe and Victor were in company with Elephant when he was shot.
COURT: Is Joe in the habit of supplying the runaways with provisions?
GERVAIS: He knows of his giving them salt and tobacco.
COURT: Do you know or did you ever see the prisoner supply the runaways with provisions?
GERVAIS: No, but I have heard it.
COURT: Did you ever see Joe in company with Elephant and the runaways?
GERVAIS: Yes I have seen him myself more than four times.

[Joe cross-examines an unnamed witness, possibly Gervais.]
JOE: When you ran away did I ever give you any salt?
WITNESS: No I never came to your house.
JOE: Did you ever see Elephant in my house?
WITNESS: I am on my oath. I have often.

Marie-Jeanne [witness] being sworn deposeth.
COURT: Do you know the prisoner?
MARIE-JEANNE: Yes I do.
COURT: Did you ever see the runaways in Joe's house?
MARIE-JEANNE: Yes I cook their victuals and held conversations.
COURT: What runaways did you ever see in Joe's house?
MARIE-JEANNE: I do not know them.
COURT: What number have you seen?
MARIE-JEANNE: Great many. They came every Friday.
COURT: Did you ever see Joe give them salt fish?
MARIE-JEANNE: I have seen him give herring and tobacco and salt with my own eyes.
COURT: Do you know how Joe got these articles?
MARIE-JEANNE: Joe leaves the runaways at his house, comes to town, buys the provisions and goes up.
COURT: What do the runaways give Joe in return for these things?
MARIE-JEANNE: Wahwahs, large panniers of them.
COURT: Did you ever see him?

MARIE-JEANNE: Yes often.
COURT: Did they ever give you anything when [missing word] were eating?
MARIE-JEANNE: No never.
COURT: What did Joe do with the wahwahs?
MARIE-JEANNE: He hides them about the houses.
COURT: What did Joe bring to town to purchase the provisions with?
MARIE-JEANNE: Wahwahs.
COURT: Nothing but wahwahs?
MARIE-JEANNE: Nothing.
COURT: How do you know that the Negroes who came to Joe's house were runaways?
MARIE-JEANNE: She [?] knows them to be so from their rush baskets and haversacks (in French *content*[8]) and cutlasses.
COURT: Is there any estate below where the Negroes could come from?
MARIE-JEANNE: No, this is the highest and last estate next the woods.
COURT: When they left Joe's house did they go up or down?
MARIE-JEANNE: They went up into the woods after putting on their *contents*.
COURT: Did ever Joe say from where he brought the provisions in town?
MARIE-JEANNE: He never told but he came to town to buy them in the market.
COURT: On the day that Elephant was killed did not Joe come to town with two runaway Negroes?
MARIE-JEANNE: Yes.

[Joe cross-examines Marie-Jeanne.]
JOE: The Sunday I came down what time did I come down?
MARIE-JEANNE: In the afternoon after you stole the tannias and potatoes to give your wife.
JOE: When I was sick in the house did you ever see the runaways come to see me?
MARIE-JEANNE: Yes, yes every day, you cooked victuals and eat them together.
JOE: Did you ever see the runaways in my house?

MARIE-JEANNE: Yes with my own eyes.

The court being cleared proceeded to take into consideration the charges of the prisoner and the evidence in support of it and of opinions that the charge is proved and ***do sentence him to be hanged*** in the market place in Roseau.
WW GLANVILLE, JUDGE ADVOCATE
DANIEL CONSTABLE, PRESIDENT

The sentence I approve and order it to be put in execution as soon as possible the head cut off and body burned as before.
GEO R AINSLIE, GOVERNOR (CO 71/51)

The TRIAL of GABRIEL

GABRIEL, belonging to Titre Duberseau, charged with being found robbing the Negro grounds of Curry's Rest and that he threatened to kill Marie Louise being in her ground.

Marie Louise being sworn that she went into her ground at 11 o'clock. She meet the same Negro Gabriel, she asked him where he came from, he answered he belong to Mr Charurier. She told him this is not Mr Charurier's – saying so she put her hand upon his breast. He fell down backwards. He had a bayonet in his hand which he presented at her. When he did so she gave him a blow with a cutlass, when he saw his blood falling he presented his bayonet again at her. When he presented this bayonet she called out for assistance and he ran away and she after him. John Louis being sworn that he heard Marie Louise call out, he ran after the prisoner and caught him. He had a quantity of clothes and a pass.[9] The prisoner denied the charge

The court being cleared proceeded to take into consideration the charge against him and the evidence in support of it are of opinion that the same is proved and do sentence him to 100 lashes in the market place in Roseau.

WW GLANVILLE , JUDGE ADVOCATE
DANIEL CONSTABLE, PRESIDENT

Dr Clarke gave in the charge the man is not tried as a runaway. I beg to observe that the proceedings ought to be revised to be tried as a runaway - Geo W Ainslie.
Gabriel charged and ordered by the Governor to be tried as a runaway.

John Louis [witness] being sworn
COURT: Do you know him?
JOHN LOUIS: No.
COURT: Did you ever see him before you took him up?
JOHN LOUIS: No. It is the first time I ever saw him.
COURT: Is he a runaway?
JOHN LOUIS: The prisoner told him he was runaway.
COURT: How long?
JOHN LOUIS: Since New Year's Day.

The prisoner being asked what he had to say – that his master never fed him, put iron on his feet.

The court being cleared were of opinion that he is guilty by his confessions to the witness when taken but it appears that he has only been absent since the first day of January last, I do sentence him to be worked in the galley gang for three months in addition to the 100 lashes sentenced to be inflicted upon him.
WW GLANVILLE, JUDGE ADVOCATE
DANIEL CONSTABLE, PRESIDENT
Approved *GEO R AINSLIE*. Let him witness the capital criminal. (CO 71/51)

12 MARCH 1814
This extract from the Dominica Journal, dateline Roseau, reported on the latest developments in Ainslie's campaign against the Maroons.

The perseverance of those employed under His Excellency's directions, in harassing the runaway slaves, continues to be crowned with almost daily success. Yesterday the head of a runaway Negro, belonging to Betsey Wallace[10], was sent in by the Dominica Rangers, from Layon [sic]. He was shot while pillaging the provisions in the camp called Noel. One of his comrades, who is said to have been runaway 17 years, was taken and detained for a guide; another escaped being taken, but is supposed to have fallen down a precipice.[11]

Sunday 13 MARCH 1814
The TRIALS of HESTER, FRANCOISE, REGISTE, PERINE, JENNY and BETTY

Another court martial was held in which six women were found guilty, of whom two were sentenced to hang. Women featured in marronage throughout the Caribbean. Of the 577 Maroons officially listed as killed, taken and surrendered between May 1813 and November 1814, 194 were women representing nearly one third of those taken while 78 were children. Like the men, the women left the estates for a variety of reasons, such as cruelty and overwork. Many, also like the men, were in the forests for many years. In the trials, some women defendants told the court that they had wanted to return to the plantations but had been stopped by the men.[12] *They were often accompanied by children. There are no known women chiefs in this period but Sarah of Hillsborough was certainly a leader* (*see page 46*).

Proceedings of a court martial held on the 13th day of March 1814, by order of His Excellency GR Ainslie Governor and Commander in Chief for the trials of such prisoners as may be brought before them. President. Lieutenant Colonel Armatrading, St George's; Captain Robinson, St Paul's, Captain Bevis, St George's; Lieutenant Robinson, St George's, Lieutenant Dodds, Lieutenant Watson, St Paul's; Ensign Gloster, St George's. The court being sworn by the Judge Advocate, and the Judge Advocate having been sworn by the President.

HESTER and her two children named [words missing], **FRANCOISE** and **REGISTE** belonging to Mrs Myler, **PERINE** belonging to Mrs Powel, **JENNY** belonging to Mr Greg and **BETTY** belonging to Mrs Warner charged with having absented themselves from their owners' employment and with being taken in the camp of the runaways by a party of Dominica Rangers.

Charlemagne, a volunteer, in the Dominica Rangers being sworn deposed that he and Mr Martial Robin set off the day before yesterday with 10 privates of the Rangers and four guides and 14 pioneers. The runaway slave who had been taken the other day took us to the place where the prisoners had taken refuge. When we got up we found the little boy prisoner digging wahwahs. The guide rolled down a stone at him and he bawled out, "Don't hurt me," thinking we were runaways as he was. I being in front cried out to him to halt. He did so. When the others heard that they all ran away tho Capt Mr Robin desired them to pursue them the witness and the two guides ran after them. I took three. Another private took the prisoner Hester and her two children, the other prisoners were also secured by different soldiers, a private took three muskets, one of which was loaded close to a *content*, which had two Carib baskets [illegible word] which had all the clothes of the captain of camp named John. Three women made their escape. He came down with the prisoners nine in number.

Lamba [?] Count [Court?], being sworn deposed that when the party went up after the runaways he found the man had gone away leaving the women to watch their baskets. They chased the men who had got away. They took three muskets, two Indian baskets full of clothes. The party took all the prisoners now before the court. He came down to town with them. Hester being asked if she had any questions said no, the man who took her cried out to her to stop and she did so.

The other prisoners declined asking any questions.

The prisoner Hester acknowledged she ran away about a month before the French attacked the island[13]. Francoise being asked how long she had runaway about two years. Jenny said she ran away about three months that she had a sore leg and got a pass from the manager to get her leg cured by [illegible word] in town, that she was in Roseau in the hurricane and went back to get her pass renewed and in going back she was met by a Negro who said he would take her to Castle Bruce to get her leg cured,

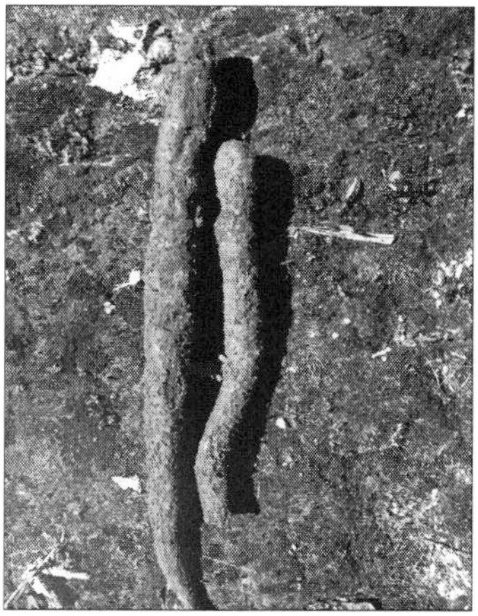

Wahwah, the indigenous wild yam (Rajania cordata), *was an important source of food for the Maroons and was traded for goods such as salt and guns. Right: the wahwah vine is still found in some areas of Dominica, in particular, the east.*

that he took her into the woods, where she has been ever since til taken by the party of Dominica Rangers.

Perine being asked what she had to say said she runaway since the last Christmas that she was punished by the manager who put a chain round her neck because her husband had runaway and she went to join her husband in the woods.

Betty being asked how long she had been runaway said she had been absent about a year that she ran away the Xmas before the last.

The court being cleared are of the opinion the charges proved against the prisoners Hester, Francoise, Perine, Jenny and Betty and do ***sentence Hester who appears to be with child to be remanded to prison until she be delivered and then to be hanged***[14]***. The prisoner Francoise to be hanged.*** Perine 50 lashes and to be worked in the chain gang for three months. The prisoners Jenny and Betty to be discharged in consequence of their very

bad states of health, and they acquit Registe and the other children.
WW GLANVILLE
EG ARMATRADING, PRESIDENT AND LIEUTENANT COLONEL, ROYAL ST GEORGE'S REGIMENT OF DOMINICA MILITIA

I approve and direct the execution to take place immediately, the head after hanging two hours to be struck off fixed on a pike and the body burnt at 4 o'clock. *GEO R AINSLIE* (CO 71/51)

19 MARCH 1814

The Dominica Journal reported on the trials of Hester and Francoise, alongside news about the surrender of two army deserters, one white, the other black, and the destruction of another Maroon camp. White runaways from the British army - deserters from the "concentration camps of the garrison and the hovering, fearsome plagues".[15] *- sometimes joined the Maroons in the forests. John Elvin (below) was one of them. The Observer newspaper in London, England, reprinted the article on May 22.*

The operations against the Maroons continue to be crowned with almost daily success, and hold the prospect of a speedy termination to their nefarious practices. On Saturday last, five women and four children were sent in; two of the women were put on their trial, convicted of being notorious offenders and received sentence of death. One of them (Francoise, belonging to Madame Eynard) was executed pursuant to her sentence on Sunday last; but the other (Esther [Hester], belonging to Mr Menier) being pregnant, was respited during His Excellency's pleasure.

On Wednesday a deserter from the 60th regiment, named John Elvin, who has been long absent with the runaways, surrendered himself. And yesterday Hypolite, a black deserter from the 4th West India Regt, and a number of runaway slaves, gave themselves up.

The private camp of the chief, Louis Mocho [sic], has been discovered and destroyed; a great quantity of baggage, poultry, stock, furniture etc etc carried away by volunteer Vidal, with a party of the Rangers.

Sunday 27 MARCH 1814
The TRIALS of FLORA, ADELAIDE and CAROLINE

Three more women runaways were put on trial, one of whom, a woman called Adelaide, was hanged. The trial reveals reasons why the women had run away - because of "misery and sickness", said Caroline. The evidence also provides detail of life in the Maroon camps for women and children. All three women said that they had wanted to surrender but that the camp chiefs had stopped them.

Proceedings of a court martial held by virtue of an order of His Excellency GR Ainslie, Governor in Chief in and over the said island, and on Sunday the 27th day of March 1814 for the trial of such prisoners as may be brought before us. Lieutenant Col Armatrading; Captain Lewthwaite, Captain Jacquin; Lieutenant Laing, Lieutenant Matthews; Ensign Glanville, Ensign Nightingale [all of Royal St George's Regiment except Nightingale from St Paul's]; WW Glanville, Judge Advocate.

The President and members having been sworn by the President the following prisoners, **FLORA**, **ADELAIDE** and **CAROLINE** accused of being runaway from their owners and with being taken in the camp of the runaways.

Germain, Private with Loyal Dominica Rangers, being sworn. He and one of this party commanded by the Sergeant Major was present when the prisoners were taken when they went to the camp a little boy saw them and cried out white men are coming and plenty of soldiers. They all ran away but they chase them and took two prisoners, Adelaide and Caroline in the camp. We saw no men, we took one musket after they had taken the two prisoners and the mulatto woman's child, Flora, she came and surrendered to the party there were taken in the whole the three prisoners, three small children and the boy who gave the alarm.

Baptiste, a Private in the Loyal Dominica Rangers being sworn, they proceeded to the runaway camp commanded by the Sergeant Major they went up and he heard a boy cry out, "Look, white people", and the

Negroes in the camp began to run. They came up to the camp and the Sergeant Major sent them into the bushes to try and catch them. One of the party took Adelaide and Caroline; the boy who gave the alarm was taken by Germain the last witness. The children were taken up by the two P [prisoners] but when the party began to fire they stopped and were made prisoners. There was one child asleep in the camp which they took; the prisoner Flora knowing the camp to be taken came and surrendered herself not being desirous of going any further they took a musket and a bottle and half of powder.

The prisoner Adelaide being asked what she had to say, answered she does not know how long she has been in the woods, she had been a year; she asked the Captain to let her come down but he would not. The last time the Governor offered pardon to all those who would come back she made an agreement with a boy, then in the camp to runaway. She set off with him from the camp and three days afterwards she was found by the party who had been sent after her. She was brought back to the camp and tied there until they took everyone that had got away and until they found Jacko who had by some means lost himself; when they found Jacko they let her go. One of the guides in the woods knows this to be true that she did not runaway when the party of the Rangers came up she said she tried to get away from the camp but they could not.

Caroline being asked what she had to offer in her defence said she had been absent about five years, that she was in Quashie's camp, that she tried to escape but they would not let them. Being asked what made her runaways said misery and sickness.

Flora being asked what she had to say that she was quite little when she ran away, her master gave her some thing to carry to the Bay and she fell down and lost them. When she came to the house her master gave her a flogging. She went away and met an old man who took her to the woods and she has been there since, that she frequently tried to get away but without success. She said she surrendered because the child was taken. She had been to get mountain cabbages but she heard firing and as soon as the firing was over she surrendered to the party.

The court being cleared proceeded to take into consideration the charges against the prisoners and are of opinion they are guilty of the same, and ***do sentence the prisoner Adelaide to be hung,*** Caroline to be worked in the chain gang until she can be banished from the island and the P [prisoner] Flora to be worked in the chain gang until she can be banished from the island.
WW GLANVILLE, JUDGE ADVOCATE
EG ARMATRADING, ROYAL ST GEORGE'S REGIMENT, DOMINICA MILITIA, PRESIDENT

Approved and ordered to be carried into immediate effect in the manner heretofore.
GEOG R AINSLIE, GOVERNOR (CO 71/51)

Sunday 3 APRIL 1814
The TRIALS of ZABET, EBO and REBECCA

Proceedings of a court martial held by order of His Excellency, GR Ainslie, Governor and Commander in Chief in and over the island on the 3rd day of April for the trial of such prisoners as may be brought before them. President, Major Constable, St George's Regiment; Captain Robinson, St Paul's, Captain Grano, St Luke's, Captain Henderson, St George's; Lieutenant McCorry, St Paul's, Lieutenant Etang, St Luke's, Lieutenant Keay, St George's; Judge Advocate, WW Glanville. The President and members having been sworn by the Judge Advocate and the Judge Advocate having been sworn by the President, the following prisoners were brought before the court.

ZABET [or Zabeth], belonging to Mr Marceau, and **EBO** [or Vielle Ebo] belonging to Mr Marceau. Vielle Ebo charged with being runaway 10 years and practising witchcraft and taken in a runaway camp.

Charlemagne being sworn deposed that they went from Prince Rupert's after the runaways. They went up very high in the heights of Bois Pilot, when they came there they heard somebody digging wahwahs. It was too late and they waited the next morning. In the morning we got into their huts we shot one and took eight, among them was the prisoner. They found the old woman on her bed having materials about her for the purpose of practising witchcraft.

Basile, a Private in the Loyal Dominica Rangers, being sworn deposed that he went up with the other witness and found the P [prisoner] asleep; that she awoke and ran and they ran after her and took her. They took the materials for practising witchcraft hanging up in her house near to her bed.

The prisoner being asked what she had to say in her defence, said the party came and found them asleep. They fired a musket. They got up and ran. They shot the man who had the materials for witchcraft. That Charlemagne put them into her hand. She had been absent about three years that her master put her to watch cane and some of them were missing and she ran away.

REBECCA and Zabet belonging to Mr Marceau charged with having been absent, the former four years and the latter one year and with being taken in the runaway camp.

Charlemagne being again sworn that the party of Rangers went up as before, stated in his former disposition that they took Zabet asleep and Rebecca came and surrendered about an hour afterwards.

Basile being sworn deposed that he was one of the party sent after the runaways. They took Zabet and the former prisoner and Rebecca came and surrendered afterwards.

Zabet being asked what she had to say, acknowledged that she was in Jacko's camp and was working with the old woman. Rebecca said she was in Jacko's camp and taken with the others.

The court being cleared proceeded to take into consideration the charges preferred against the prisoners and the evidence in support of them and one of opinion that the prisoner Vielle [Ebo] is not guilty of the charge of practising witchcraft, in as much as no evidence had been produced in support of it, but do find her guilty of having been runaway

and with being taken in the runaway camp and *do sentence her to be hanged,* at such time and place as the Governor may appoint. They also find that Zabet and Rebecca were guilty of the charges preferred upon them and *do sentence them to be hanged.*
MR GLANVILLE, JUDGE ADVOCATE,
MAJOR CONSTABLE, ROYAL ST GEORGE'S REGIMENT, PRESIDENT

Approved and ordered the sentences against Vielle Ebo and Rebecca to be carried into immediate execution.[16] *GEO R AINSLIE, GOVERNOR* (CO 71/51)

Saturday 9 APRIL 1814
The TRIAL of ANDREW WARNER

Proceedings of a court martial held by order of His Excellency Governor Ainslie on the 9th day of April 1814 during martial law for the trial of such prisoners as may be brought before themselves

President, Lieut Col Armatrading, Royal St George's; Captain Bevis, Royal St George's, Captain Grano, St Luke's; Lieutenant Holmes, St George's, Lieutenant Court, St George's, Lieutenant Watson, St Paul's; Ensign Gloster, St George's.

ANDREW WARNER charged with holding intercourse with the runaways to which the prisoner pleaded not guilty.

Shaw, belonging to Hillsborough estate, being sworn knows the prisoner who lives at old Warner's estate. The prisoner gave the gun (now produced) to a Negro belonging to Hillsborough estate named Abraham, a runaway Negro now in the woods. He, the witness and Abraham were in the camp together, Abraham gave the prisoner plantains in exchange for the gun. He carried him plantains four times, that he saw him carry the plantains, that Abraham brought the gun into the camp and told him he had brought it from Andrew, that he never saw the gun in the possession of the prisoner, that he has once been on Mt George estate, that he never saw the gun in the prisoner's possession but Abraham told him that the gun was Andrew's, that he once went to Andrew's house, that he never saw the gun in his house but he once brought plantains, Andrew gave him nothing, that he has seen the gun in the hands of the prisoner. He was not there when he sold the gun, that he has been in the prisoner's house three times since he ran away, he carried plantains the times he went, that he gave them to the prisoner and he in return gave him a glass of rum and salt to carry with them, that he never gave him anything else, that he was not there when the gun was sold, that he gave a man named Ochra, a runaway, tobacco to give to Abraham, that he saw him give the man the tobacco and at the same time told him not to let the Negroes see him.

Q Did you ever see Andrew give powder?
A No I never did.
Q Did you ever see him give anything else?
A No.
He never saw the prisoner sell cutlasses but was present and saw him put a handle to a cutlass which he gave to a man of the name of Cuffy to give to Abraham.

That Andrew, the prisoner, and the others who came with him were runaways, that salt he gave them was for Abraham, that Abraham otherwise called John is a chief, that he only gave them salt once.
The prisoner being asked if he had questions to ask:
Q Were you present when I put the handle on the cutlass?
A No I was not. I was present when Cuffy gave the cutlass to Andrew from Abraham and begged him to put a handle on the same, when they returned he gave the cutlass to Cuffy.

The prisoner further stated that the gun was given him by his master a few days after the hurricane; he went to the bay to bring up lumber for his mistress he found this house broke open, all his clothes, baskets, pots, pans and everything and the gun carried away. That he immediately gave notice of it to his mistress and to all the neighbourhood. The witness being asked if he knew anything of the robbing, answered he did, that it was done by one of their own Negroes who is runaway and carried another gun into the woods longer than the one produced.

Betty belonging to Mrs Warner being sworn remember when [illegible words] brought a gun into the woods.

The court being cleared were of opinion that the charge is partly proved against him and do therefore sentence him to be banished from the island though he be worked in chains until [he] can be sent from the colony.
WW GLANVILLE, JUDGE ADVOCATE
EG ARMATRADING, LIEUTENANT COLONEL ROYAL ST GEORGE'S REGIMENT, DOMINICA MILITIA, PRESIDENT

The court martial in obedience to His Excellency's directions to that effect proceeded to reconsider the sentence awarded against the prisoner Andrew and after maturely and deliberately reconsidering the same do not think the evidence sufficient to convict him capitally of the crime of which he is accused.
WW GLANVILLE JUDGE ADVOCATE
E GEO ARMATRADING, LIEUTENANT COLONEL, ROYAL ST GEORGE'S REGIMENT, DOMINICA MILITIA, PRESIDENT (CO 71/51)

The TRIALS of JULIEN, JANE and SELIMENE

JULIEN, **JANE** and **SELIMENE** taken up as runaways.
Charlemagne, Sergeant in the Loyal Dominica Rangers. He went with a party after the runaways commanded by the Sergeant Major. They saw him digging wahwah, [they] chased the prisoner Julien the whole night. They followed the traces of his footsteps. They got to his ajoupa in the woods about daylight when they went in he was asleep. When he awoke and saw them, he got up and ran. They pursued until one of the party gave him a cut on the head and took him.

John, Corporal in the LD Rangers, being sworn. He went with a party commanded by Mr Vidal. The party went to a camp commanded by Noel. They got into the camp about the time that had done dinner. They fired into the camp and killed one woman and took the two women Jane and

Selimene and three children. They tried to make their escape. They fired at them and wounded one of them named Jane. The camp was commanded by Noel. He know him. He fired and wounded one of the sergeants and that he got wounded. They picked up a small calabash of powder and a bag of bullets, a trunk and a hat belonging to the late Mr McFarlane.

The prisoner Julien being asked what he had to say says he belonged to Mr Dubuc. The overseer made him runaway he has run away about two years.

Jane being also asked the reason she runaway was her mistress gave her two bills to buy sugars for one of the other Negroes. She lost the money and went away. She had no idea of going in the woods, but was made fool of by a Negro, that she tried to escape but was taken and flogged.

Selimene being asked. She tried to get away but could not. She had been absent about 18 months. She belongs to Gibon's estate. The runaway Negroes came down to the bayside and conducted her to the camp.

The court being cleared are of the opinion that the prisoners are guilty of the charge preferred against them and do sentence them to receive 39 lashes in the market place and to be worked in chains until they can be banished.

WW GLANVILLE, JUDGE ADVOCATE
E GEO ARMATRADING, LIEUTENANT COLONEL, ROYAL ST GEORGE'S DOMINICA MILITIA, PRESIDENT
approved *GEO R AINSLIE GOVERNOR* dismiss the court (CO 71/51)

11 APRIL 1814

The Times newspaper in England reported on the war against the Maroons in Dominica, described it as "sanguinary warfare" and mentioned the "atrocious orders" of Ainslie's proclamation. It stated that it does not know whether "these atrocious orders" were acted upon.

A most sanguinary warfare has for some months past been waged in the island of Dominica, against the runaway slaves, who had sought refuge in the woods, and the Maroons by whom they were harboured and protected. At an early period of the contest, the Governor, it is said, issued a proclamation, promising pardon to such of the runways as surrendered themselves within a specified period; and denounced to those who did not take the benefit of this act of amnesty, that "The Rangers had orders to take no prisoners, but put to death men, women and children, without exceptions." We know not whether these atrocious orders were literally fulfilled.

20 APRIL 1814

Moco George, a chief, belonging to Mr Blondel, was killed by the Loyal Dominica Rangers.

30 APRIL 1814

Another chief, Gabriel, whose titular owner was unknown, was killed by the Loyal Dominica Rangers.

3 MAY 1814

The TRIAL of MICHEL

Proceedings of a court martial held by virtue of an order from His Excellency GR Ainslie Capt General and Governor in Chief of this island on third day of May 1814 for the trial of such prisoners brought to them. Lieutenant Col E G Armatrading, Royal St George's Regiment; Captain Bertrand, St David's, Captain Simpson, St Andrew's, Captain Sydenham, St Andrew's; Lieutenant Denbow, St Andrew's, Lieutenant Dodds, Royal St George's Regiment, Lieutenant Keay, Royal St George's Regiment.

MICHEL, belonging to Mr Charurier, charged with having been a runaway and having been absent about seven years taken in a camp.

John Charurier being sworn deposed that the prisoner had been absent since the 1st October 1805. He has been informed that the prisoner said he would never return until his master's eyes were closed, that he was the second in command in one of the camps.

Good Luck, belonging to Mr Charurier, being sworn deposed that he knows the prisoner, that he belongs to Mr Charurier, that he was in Louis

Moco's camp with him [and] when the chief of the camp was absent the prisoner took command.

That he has learned from others that the prisoner said he never would return until his master's eyes were closed, that he the witness was three years in the camp and that the prisoner was in the same camp with him during the whole of that time. He does not know of his endeavouring to inveigle the other Negroes from the estate. That he never had any quarrel with the prisoner.

Sydney belonging to Mr Chaurier being sworn deposed that the last witness told him that the prisoner had said he never would return until his master's eyes were closed.

Charlemagne, of the LD Rangers, being sworn that he found the prisoner covering [?] a small hut in Quashie's camp. After he saw the party of Rangers the prisoner ran. They chased him, fired at him, and called upon him to stop, which he did. They went into Quashie's camp and found four muskets, powder and shot.

The prisoner being called upon for his defence could offer nothing by way of excuse for his absence.

The TRIAL of LOUISONNE

LOUISONNE [missing word] to Mr Charurier charged with being a runaway and absent two years and taken in a camp.

John Charurier deposed that the prisoner the last time she ran away was on the 4th October 1810 and has been absent ever since.

Charlemagne being again sworn deposed that he was one of the party who took the prisoner. That she ran away when they got into Quashie's camp. The party chased her and called out to her when she stopped. The prisoner in her defence said it was not her master made her runaway but the Negroes induced her to go. Mr Charurier said that she was quite a child when she went away and believes was enticed away by a man of the name of Warner. The prisoner being asked why she did not surrender says she was prevented by the captain of the camp Quashie.

The TRIALS of EUGENIE, FLORA, MADGE, SANDRINE, LISETTE and ANGELIQUE

EUGENIE, **FLORA**, **MADGE**, **SANDRINE**, **LISETTE** and **ANGELIQUE**, charged with being runaway and taken in a camp.

Charlemagne being again sworn deposed that all the prisoners were taken by the party of the Rangers in the same camp.

The prisoners being asked for their defence and why they did not return said they could not, the men would not let them. Flora said she belongs to Mr Marceau, says that she was picking castor seeds when a man named Cuffee took her up.

Mr Simpson stated that Madge had been absent since 1799.

Alexandrine [Sandrine] said she has been absent about two years.

Lisette said she has been absent three years and belongs to Mr Hartaut that her mistress beat her and she went away.

Eugenie says she belongs to Mrs Boland and has been absent about one year, that she went away because her mistress ordered her to sweep the yard at night.

Angelique belongs to SM Daroux, says she has been absent about one year.

The court being cleared to take into consideration the charges against the prisoners and the evidence in support of them are of [the] opinion that the prisoner Michel is guilty and *do sentence him to be hanged and that his head be struck off and put upon Hertford Bay opposite Mr Charurier stores.*

The court are of opinion that the charges are also proved against the women and do sentence Louisonne to be banished from the island and to be worked in the chain gang until she be banished.

Flora to be banished and to be worked in the chain gang until she be banished, Eugenie to be banished and to be worked in the chain gang until banished; Madge in consideration of her being a new Negro when she ran away and of her being taken away by force to receive 39 lashes in the market place and to be banished and to be worked with chain gang until banished; Sandrine to be banished and to be confined in jail until she be banished; Lisette to be banished and to be worked in the chain gang until she be banished; Angelique to be worked in the chain gang until banished.

WW GLANVILLE, JUDGE ADVOCATE

EG ARMATRADING, LT COL R ST GEORGE'S REGIMENT, DOMINICA MILITIA, PRESIDENT

Approve and order the sentence to be put in immediate execution.

GEO R AINSLIE, GOVERNOR (CO 71/51)

7 MAY 1814

The Scots Magazine, with the dateline Roseau, Dominica, 7 May, reported on successful attacks on Maroon camps and the capture and trial of women runaways. It also described in some detail the defences erected around the Maroon camps - sharp wooden stakes concealed in deep pits.

The exertions used to suppress the Maroons, continue with unabated vigour, and continued success: 21 runaways were sent into town on Thursday: they belonged to Quasbey's [sic] private camp, which was taken, and destroyed, by a detachment of the Dominica Rangers, under volunteer Vidal. In this camp was found 24 houses or large huts, four loaded muskets, and some powder, a great deal of clothing, a few dollars, and a considerable number of poultry, which of course became the property of the Colonial Rangers.

The same night intelligence was received from Captain Savarin of the capture of George Moco's[17] camp near the Trois Pitons, the chief and two others were killed, their heads taken off, and stuck up at Portsmouth. This party was in pursuit of the remaining fugitives. A woman and two children were also taken and sent to town on Thursday.

Scarcely a day passes that Maroon women and children, and runaway slaves, are not brought for trial and punishment. Many of the former declare they were born in the woods, and never saw a white man until the moment of their apprehension. During the last five weeks a great number of females have been tried by military commissions, condemned, executed and their heads cut off.

It has been discovered to guard against surprise, they surround their camps with deep pits into which stakes with pointed tops are driven. They also drive sharp pieces of wood and bone into the footpaths. If, on the first alarm of their scouts, the strangers cannot bring down the fugitives, they dare not pursue until the road be explored, lest they should fall into the pits and be staked alive or crippled by treading on the footpaths. In the meanwhile the Maroons, to whom certain bypaths are also known, escape with their families.

Two soldiers belonging to the 4th West India Regiment, named Somers and Hypolite, were shot in Church Savannah, at New Town, for deserting and taking refuge in the woods amongst the Maroons.[18]

Sunday 22 MAY 1814
The TRIALS of QUASHIE, MILLS and BEAUTY

The final court martial had three defendants: Beauty of Belfast estate, and Quashie and Mills, of Woodford Hill estate, all of whom were charged with "holding intercourse" with the runaways. Quashie (a different person from the chief also named Quashie) was convicted and hanged. Quashie's death would later (see page 134) be the subject of debate in the British parliament and correspondence between Governor Ainslie and Bathurst.

Proceedings of a court martial held by virtue of an order from His Excellency GR Ainslie Captain General and Governor in Chief in and over the said island, Chancellor Vice Admiral and Ordinary of the same this 22nd day of May 1814 for the trial of such prisoners as may be brought before them. President, Major Constable, Royal St George's Regiment; Captain Labadie, Captain Jacquin, Lieutenant Hayter, Lieutenant Minette, all of Royal St George's Regiment, Lieutenant McCorry, St Paul's IC [Independent Company] and Ensign Sorando, St Luke's IC [Independent Company]

BEAUTY, Apollo's wife, **QUASHIE** of Woodford Hill, **MILLS** charged with holding intercourse with the runaways.

Robin, belonging to Woodbridge's estate, being sworn deposed that one of Quashie's master's Negroes named Casimir brought him the witness down to Quashie's house. He brought down some crapeaux[19] to Quashie and he gave him salt, saltfish and mackerel. This took place when Mr Philpots managed the estate. The next time he was brought down by Casimir he took him to Mills's house and Mills gave him salt and saltfish and a bottle of rum in exchange for some crapeaux given to him. This took place once when the witness was with him, but Casimir has frequently brought up things. He never saw Casimir bring up gunpowder. He once saw a bottle full. Apollo had powder, and since the witness was with him, the prisoner Beauty brought up some, the prisoner Beauty was Apollo's wife last year but not now.

Apollo brought the witness to Beauty's house three times that they both eat and drank in her house and he slept there three nights at different times, that he stayed there all Saturday and Sunday night, he went up when everybody was in bed, that he saw her give Apollo powder, that he saw him give her money to buy the powder, but he cannot tell how much, that she gave the powder on the Sunday night, that she was absent from her house from Saturday to Sunday night, that he saw Beauty give Apollo rum, sugar and salt. That he has brought down provision to the prisoner Beauty's house, tannias, yams and other ground provision which was given to her to sell.

Cross-examined by Quashie:

QUASHIE: Are you certain that Casimir came to my house and gave me crapeaux and did I give him in exchange salt, saltfish and mackerel?

ROBIN: Yes.

QUASHIE: When you and Casimir came to my house what did I tell you?

ROBIN: Yes. We came in the night the prisoner was in the house and a light and had a kind of a flute playing upon. Casimir called to him to open the door. He opened the door, we went in and shut the door – three of us – the first thing he offered us was rum. He boiled salt fish and plantains and gave us to eat. Casimir brought out crapeaux and two agoutis and gave him.

By the court:
COURT: Did the prisoner Quashie know you were runaways?
ROBIN: Yes he did.

By the prisoner:
QUASHIE: When did I know you? Did I know you before Mr Simpson brought you to the estate?
ROBIN: Yes you knew me long before.
QUASHIE: When Casimir gave me the crapeaux did I tell him to come back again?
ROBIN: No you paid him off in salt, saltfish and mackerel.
QUASHIE: When I gave it to him did he tell me thank you.
ROBIN: To be sure after you gave him salt.

By the court:
COURT: Did Casimir say he was coming back again?
ROBIN: Yes and the prisoner told him to come when he liked but to take care of the other Negroes and come straight to his house.
COURT: Did you know if Apollo went to his house?
ROBIN: No.

By the prisoner:
QUASHIE: When I told Casimir to come back and take care of himself, what did he say?
ROBIN: Yes he would and you gave him liberty to go to his ground and eat plantains.
QUASHIE: When I told him so what did he say?
ROBIN: You told him when he was hungry then [?] was his provision ground to go and cut what he wanted and he said, yes.

Cross-examined by Mills:
MILLS: When you and Casimir came to my ground what part was it?

ROBIN: The old ground next the door. You brought me victuals and some grog and I was waiting for you.
MILLS: Did you ever see Casimir in my case[20]?
ROBIN: No he left me in the ground and went up and said he had been to your house. You brought in victuals and we both eat of them.

By the court:
COURT: Did the prisoner Mill[s] know that you and Casimir were runaways?
ROBIN: Yes he did.
COURT: Why did you work the prisoner's ground?
ROBIN: He said he would give me some provision but he had not the time but he would come and bring it on the Sunday and we worked for it.
COURT: Did he ask Casimir to come back?
ROBIN: No I [he?] did not. He paid him off.
COURT: Did he ever come back?
ROBIN: No I believe not.

Cross-examined by Beauty:
BEAUTY: Since this Governor came here did you ever know me supply the runaways?
ROBIN: No. Since this Governor came here her husband never come down.
BEAUTY: Did you ever see me bring gunpowder?
ROBIN: I did myself.

Pierre [witness]
COURT: Do you know the prisoner?
PIERRE: Yes. Her name is Beauty and I have been twice with Apollo to her house.
COURT: Do you know her to be Apollo's wife?
PIERRE: Yes.
COURT: When was this?
PIERRE: Before Christmas last.
COURT: Is she Apollo's wife now?
PIERRE: No. She has left him.

COURT: Do you know her reason for leaving him?
PIERRE: No, I do not.
COURT: Did you ever see Beauty give Apollo powder?
PIERRE: No, I never did.
COURT: When you were at Apollo's house did you see Robin?
PIERRE: Yes, once.
COURT: When you went with Robin to Beauty house what did you bring from camp?
PIERRE: Plantains and tanias. Both Robin and myself. There were four of us.
COURT: To whom did you give them? To the prisoners?
PIERRE: Yes.
COURT: What did you receive in payment?
PIERRE: About four quarts of salt. Apollo was with us at the same time.
COURT: What did you receive the second time?
PIERRE: Tobacco.
COURT: Did you ever know the prisoner to go with Apollo to the camp.
PIERRE: I only heard so.

Cross-examined [by Beauty]
BEAUTY: Was it at my house you left the prisoners?
PIERRE: Yes it was.
BEAUTY: What did I give you in exchange?
PIERRE: Salt as I have stated before.
BEAUTY: You say I gave Apollo tobacco, how long since and how much?
PIERRE: It was before Xmas and about a handful.

The TRIAL of EULALIE

EULALIE, belonging to Mr Belair Motard[21], charged with having runaway. Modeste, Private in the LD Rangers, being sworn deposed that he went out in a party with the Sergeant Major and after travelling in the woods for three days they got to Balla's old camp and then they found this woman and a Negro man. They both ran and the party chased them and got hold of the woman, they fired at the man, who escaped.

Silvester Rontal, Private in the LD Rangers, being sworn on deposed that he went out with a party and took the prisoner.

Mr Motard Belair, the owner of the prisoner, deposed that she has been about 18 months runaway, that she is a very good woman, that one day he found her missing and heard that a Negro belonging to Mr Morceau named Edward enticed her away, that five of his Negroes went away at the same time.

The prisoner being asked what made her runaway said that she was put to watch cane, that some Negroes came and stole cane, she got frightened and a Negro belonging to her master named Alexander advised her to go away, he was asked if he treated her ill, no he did not.

The court being cleared proceeded to take into consideration the charges against the prisoners, are of opinion that they are guilty and so sentence the prisoner Quashie ***to be hanged*** his head cut off and fixed upon a pike at Woodford Hill estate.

They also sentence the prisoner Mills to receive 100 lashes and to be worked in chain until he be banished from the island, the prisoner Beauty to receive 100 lashes and to be worked in chain until she be banished from the island, the prisoner Eulalie to receive 39 lashes to be worked in chain for six months and to be returned her owner.

WW GLANVILLE, JUDGE ADVOCATE

DANIEL CONSTABLE, PRESIDENT, MAJOR IN THE ROYAL ST GEORGE'S REGIMENT

The sentence against Quashie is approved and to be put in immediate execution his body to be burnt and placed on a pike in the market place till evening, the lashes ordered to Beauty are suspended, Mills to be flogged.

GEOG R AINSLIE (CO 71/51)

With the execution of Quashie, martial law came to an end and the courts of special sessions resumed. William Bremner, the doctor and attorney, was one of two members of the plantocracy living in Dominica at this time, who raised the question as to the legality of Ainslie's declaration of martial law. He mused in his memoirs on how martial law operated. The other dissenting voice was Benjamin Lucas, senior member of the Council at the time. Both men said that a Council of War - as constitutionally required - had not assembled.

Both men, however, made their criticisms in 1815, after Ainslie's recall to London; no one in authority in Dominica is known to have questioned the Governor's policies at the time. Bremner wrote:

> The mode which the Governor adopted, in the outset of the operations against the runaways, of punishing those chiefs or others connected with them who were taken by the Militia or Rangers, deserves to be particularly noticed here. When he wished to try any culprits of this description capitally, he did not, as had been usual on former occasions, and as indeed the Act of the colony directed (martial law not being at this time in force), bring them before a regular tribunal, consisting of three Justices of the Peace and a jury of six respectable inhabitants – but on a Sunday morning when the Militia were accustomed to assemble for parade, he ordered two guns to be fired from Fort Young and the old flag to be hoisted there, which are the signals of general alarm; he then ordered a court martial immediately to assemble, consisting generally of only five members, officers of the St George's Regiment or of the neighbouring companies of Militia, and had the persons to be tried brought before them. The trial was for the most part short and summary, and the sentence, when agreed on by the court, was in the usual manner carried immediately to the Gov. for his approbation. When the culprit was found guilty and condemned to death, the execution was as summary as the trial, for generally the sentence was carried into effect in a couple of hours, always in the course of the day, and in one instance the culprit was carried from the place of trial directly to the gallows, a distance not exceeding 100 yards... After the sentences were carried out into full effect, or at any rate the following morning, the alarm was discharged by firing three guns and lowering the red flag.

... Such a mode of trial and punishment was certainly calculated to inspire terror, but I entertain very strong doubts of its legality. The Militia not only authorises the Gov. to fire an alarm in case of sudden and urgent public danger, and it debars him from keeping up such alarm longer than 24 hours without assembling a Council of War, which consists of the Council, Assembly, field officers of the Militia, and further enacts that martial law shall not be proclaimed without their consent. The words of the preamble of the clause, which respects martial law, are emphatic: "Whereas the appearance of urgent public danger may render martial law necessary, but whereas from experience of its bad effects it must ever be considered among the worst of evils – etc."

Now in the cases to which I allude there was no urgent public danger, still less any sudden danger; the prior danger indeed, during which martial law was not however in force, was of course in some degree diminished by the capture of the prisoners, who were then to be tried. Nor was any Council of War ever assembled in these cases without whose sanction the Act declares that martial law shall not be in force. It deserves, however, to be noticed, that the proofs of the usual laws in such cases are tedious, and that very great complaints have long existed of the irregular attendance of the justices to form such courts. How far therefore the deviation from strict law may in these instances be justified by the object in view, which certainly the compendious mode of proceeding adopted was calculated to promote, I shall not take upon me to decide positively. (WB, p153-5)

For his part, Benjamin Lucas asked some rhetorical questions about the Governor's behaviour. In this letter to Lord Bathurst, he described the law concerning the declaration of martial law and raised the possibility - although he refused to offer his own opinion - that Ainslie's conduct was illegal. By the tone of his letter, he must have thought that it was.

By the Militia law of this island, the Governor is authorised, in certain cases, to cause an alarm to be fired, on which the Militia is to assemble under arms, and a Council of Martial Law to be immediately summoned to judge of the propriety of causing martial law to be put in force: but if martial law is not proclaimed in 24 hours, the alarm ceases. And it is expressly provided that martial law shall not be declared or imposed but by the opinion and advice of a Council of War, to be composed as directed by the Act. On the 12 January 1814, martial law was regularly declared to continue in force for the space of 14 days when it ceased. But with regard to the courts martial held afterwards, it was otherwise. An alarm was fired and a red flag hoisted at the Fort early in the morning (generally Sunday), a number of officers were then summoned; the prisoners brought before them; tried; the sentence frequently carried with immediate execution and the court discharged by one or two o'clock, all on the same day.[22]

Whether slaves are amenable to such a court; whether that court was legally formed; whether they exceeded their powers... and whether the addition to the sentences of the court ordered by the Governor, were proper and legal, or not are matters for your Lordship's consideration, on which I do not presume to offer an opinion.[23]

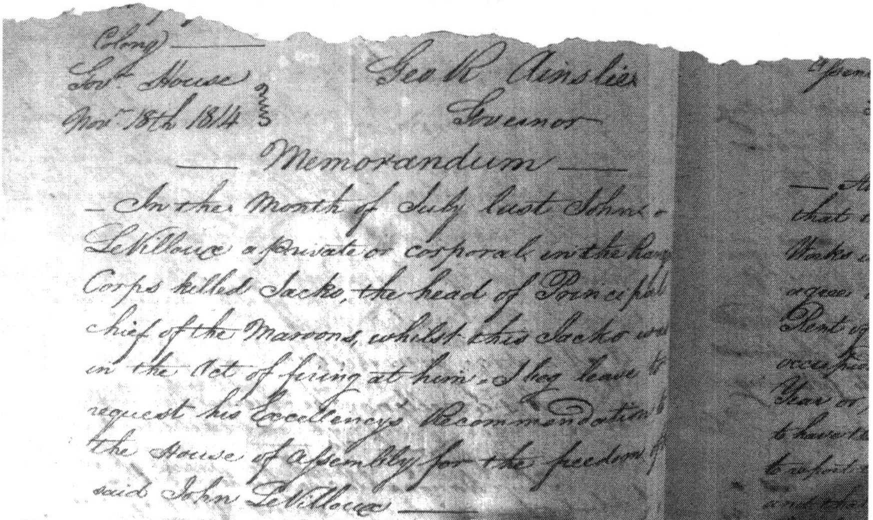
Colony
Govt. House
Nov. 18th 1814
Geo. R. Ainslie
Governor
Memorandum
— In the Month of July last John LeVilloux a Private or Corporal in the Rangers Corps killed Jacko, the head or Principal chief of the Maroons, whilst this Jacko was in the Act of firing at him — I beg leave to request his Excellency's Recommendation to the House of Assembly for the freedom of said John LeVilloux

The request from Captain Savarin for the manumission of John LeVilloux, who shot dead Chief Jacko, and (far right) as LeVilloux's name appears in the list of slaves recruited into the Dominica Rangers.

THE COURTS OF SPECIAL SESSIONS

The courts of special sessions sat again from 1 June to 25 August 1814. Fifteen more defendants were tried and one, Charlie, was executed. He was found guilty of bartering and selling salt, gunpowder and "other necessaries" to the Maroons. The first six defendants, all from Belfast estate, were found not guilty

1 JUNE 1814
The TRIALS of SCOTLAND, JOSEPH, FRANCOIS, PETER, FOX and PEGGY

At a court of special sessions held for the said island at the Court House in Roseau the 1st day of June 1814. Present the Honourable Archibald Gloster and Benjamin Lucas, William Anderson and George Garraway Esquires (Justices of the Peace), Mr W Glanville Esquire (Attorney General), Joseph Court (acting clerk of the Crown), Thomas Laing (acting Provost Marshal), Edward H Beech, interpreter.

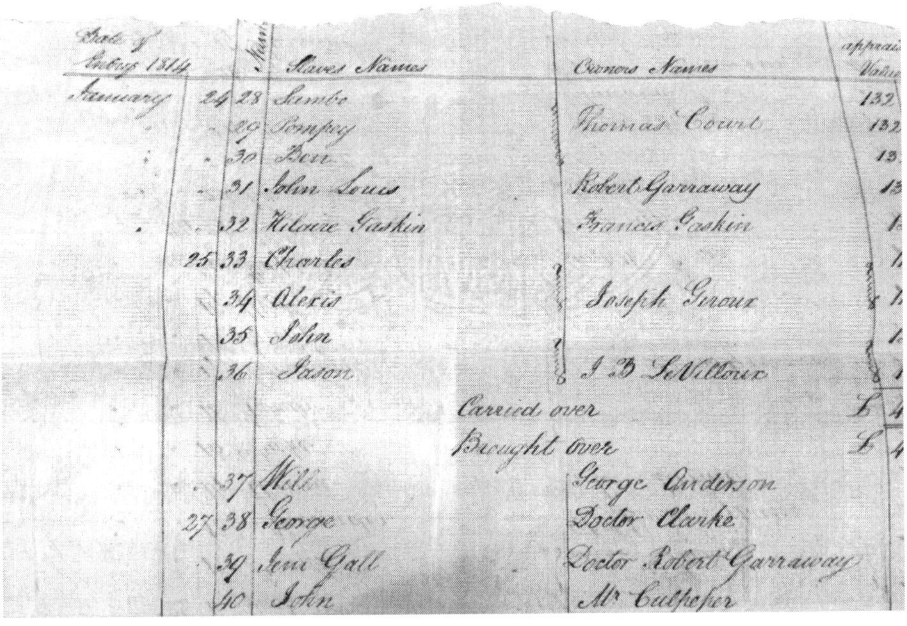

Date of [illegible] 1814		Num	Slaves Names	Owners Names	appraised Value
January	24	28	Sambo		132
		29	Pompey	Thomas Court	132
		30	Ben		13
		31	John Louis	Robert Garraway	13
		32	Hilaire Gaskin	Francis Gaskin	1
	25	33	Charles		1
		34	Alexis	Joseph Giroux	1
		35	John		1
		36	Jason	J B Sevilloux	1
			Carried over		£ 4
			Brought over		£ 4
		37	Willi[illegible]	George Anderson	
	27	38	George	Doctor Clarke	
		39	Jean Gall	Doctor Robert Garraway	
		40	John	Mr Culpeper	

SCOTLAND, **JOSEPH**, **FRANCOIS**, **PETER**, **FOX** and **PEGGY**, six Negro slaves belonging to Belfast estate, stand charged with having at various periods prior to the 23rd day of May last held intercourse or correspondence with the runaway slaves contrary to an Act of this island in such case made and provided, the prisoners having been charged with the said indictment pleaded "not guilty" whereupon a jury having been empanelled by the Provost Marshal to wit Samuel Gray, John Howell, Edward Gray, Robert Hutchings, Thomas Rawsthorn and Nathaniel Daly and having made choice of Samuel Gray as their foreman were duly sworn, and the evidence adduced on behalf of the prosecution as well as on behalf of the prisoners having been fully heard pronounced by their foreman the prisoners "not guilty" whereupon the Court ordered the prisoners to be released and their fees charged to the colony. (CO 71/51)

28 JUNE 1814

By now flushed with success, Ainslie proposed a reduction in the numbers of the Ranger Corps from the beginning of 1815. He was confident enough to suggest that ..."guides will hardly be necessary the Rangers being now so well acquainted with the woods."[24]

8 JULY 1814
The TRIAL of CHARLES

CHARLES, a Negro slave belonging to Elizabeth Moore, stands charged with having on various days and times sold and bartered gunpowder and salt and other provisions with the runaway slaves, and with having held intercourse and correspondence with them contrary to the Act in such case made and provided, the prisoner having been charged with this indictment and a jury having been empannelled by the Provost Marshal to wit Joseph Louthwaite, Francis Culpeper, Ralph Ashton, George Thomas, Charles Jones and Samuel Anderson, and having made choice of Joseph Louthwaite as their foreman were duly sworn, and the evidence adduced on behalf of the prosecution as well as on behalf of the prisoner having been fully heard pronounced by their foreman the prisoner "not guilty", he was ordered by the court to be released and his fees charged to the colony. (CO 71/51)

12 JULY 1814

In what would become a symbolic moment signalling the beginning of the end for the Maroons, Jacko, described as "the oldest chief", was killed at his camp in the Layou Valley by a Ranger called John LeVilloux. Jacko had survived in the island's hinterland for "upwards of 40 years" and his name occurs in a list of Maroon chiefs from the 1780s. His camp, described by Ainslie and others as the "Grand camp", was on the Layou Flats, a ridge surrounded on three sides by the Layou River near the community now known as Bells. This is how Thomas Southey, author of A Chronological History of the West Indies, reported Jacko's death.

Upon the 12th of July, the camp of Jacko, one of the chiefs of the Maroons at Dominica, was surprised by a party of Rangers. Jacko made a desperate resistance; he killed two Rangers, wounded a third, and was shot through the head while levelling a musket at a fourth. He had resided in the woods upwards of 40 years, and was considered chief of all the runaways.[25]

23 JULY 1814 **and 2 AUGUST** 1814
The TRIALS of ISIDOR, MARTIN, CONDO and MARIE

Dominica. At a court of special sessions held for the said island at the court house in Roseau on 23 July 1814. Present the Honourable James Clark, John Gordon, Edward H Beech Esquires (Justices of the Peace), WW Glanville Esquire (Attorney General), Joseph Court (acting clerk of the Crown), Thomas Laing (acting Provost Marshal), Edward H Beech (interpreter).

ISIDOR, belonging to Mr Roger, **MARTIN** belonging to Madame Touissant, **CONDO** belonging to Belfast estate and **MARIE**[26] belonging to Mademoiselle Jinette, severally stand charged with having absented themselves from their owner's employment for upwards of six months, contrary to an Act of this island in such case made and provided, the prisoners having been charged with this indictment pleaded "not guilty" and a jury having been empanelled by the Provost Marshal to wit Robert Stewart, Thomas St Martin, Peter Phillips, Francis Laudat, Alexander Dunbar, Henry Rhoades, and Archibald Taylor and having made the choice of Robert Stewart for their foreman were duly sworn, the court were pleased to order the prisoners to be remanded to gaol for further evidence and to be again brought up at the next court.

Isidor, Martin and Condo, were brought up and charged with having absented themselves from their owners employ for upwards of six months contrary to the Act and the prisoners having been charged with the said indictment pleaded "not guilty" and a jury having been empanelled by the Provost Marshal to wit Robert Stewart, Thomas St Martin, Peter Phillips, Francis Laudat, Alexander Dunbar, Henry Rhoades and Archibald Taylor and having made choice of Robert Stewart for their foreman were duly sworn and the evidence adduced on behalf of the prosecution as well as on the behalf of the prisoners having been fully heard pronounced by their foreman that the prisoners are "guilty", the court sentenced the said prisoners to receive each 39 lashes on the bare breech in the market place and to be banished the island. (CO 71/51)

4 AUGUST 1814

By early August, seven months after the first declaration of martial law, Ainslie reported to Lord Bathurst that his "object is nearly accomplished". Even so, Ainslie admitted that the Maroon chief, Apollo, was still at large.

I have the honour to enclose returns of Maroons, who have surrendered or been taken and pardoned since my last [illegible word]. I have not found it necessary to inflict the most trifling punishment on the prisoners, my object is nearly accomplished, and I trust that the capture of the Chief Apollo, an event at no great distance, who only escaped by a wonderful exertion of strength in a struggle latterly, when his wife and others seemed taken, will complete the tranquillisation of the interior.

NB: I know no instance of a pardoned or surrendered Maroon taking refuge again in the woods or leaving his master in any way: between 450 and 500 are now pretty well accounted for, as I may reckon at 130 surrendered Negroes whose masters failed, from disuse of the regulations, to report them. (CO 71/49)

25 AUGUST 1814
The TRIALS of CUFFY, LAFLEUR, BELINDA and CHARLIE

These were the last trials to take place during Governor Ainslie's administration.

Dominica. At a court of special sessions held for the said island at the court house in Roseau 25th August 1814. Present John Gordon, William Anderson, Edward H Beech and Thomas Henderson Esquires (Justices of the Peace), WW Glanville Esquire (Attorney General), Joseph Court (acting clerk of the Crown), Thomas Laing (acting Provost Marshal).

CUFFY, a Negro slave belonging to the estate of Captain Hall, stands charged with having absented himself from his owners employ for upwards of six months contrary to the Act in such case made and provided, the Court ordered that the said prisoner be remanded to gaol for further evidence.

LAFLEUR, a Negro slave belonging to Thomas Vidal, stands charged with having absented himself from his owners employ for upwards of six months contrary to an Act of the island in such case made and provided, the prisoner having been charged with the indictment pleaded "not guilty" and a jury having been empanelled by the Provost Marshal to wit Thomas Hayes, George Thomas, George Anderson, Dominique Long, Francis Laudat and Edward B Preston and having made a choice of Thomas Hayes as their foreman were duly sworn and the evidence adduced on behalf of the prosecution as well as the behalf of the prisoner having been fully heard pronounced by the foreman that the prisoner is "guilty" whereupon sentenced him to be worked in chains until banished from the island.

BELINDA, a Negro woman slave belonging to Mr Henderson (here Mr Henderson left the bench), stands charged with having absented herself from her owner's employ for upwards of six months contrary to an Act of the island in such case made and provided, whereupon the same jury having been empanelled by the Provost Marshal and sworn and the evidence on behalf of the prosecution as well as on behalf of the prisoner having been fully heard, pronounced by their foreman that the prisoner is "guilty" the court sentence her to be worked in chains until banished the island.
CHARLIE, a Negro slave belonging to Everton Hall estate, stands charged with having on various days and places sold, given and bartered gunpowder, fire arms, salt, salt provision and other necessaries to the runaway slaves, and with having held intercourse and correspondence with the runaway slaves contrary to an act of the island in such cases made and provided, whereupon the prisoner having been charged with the said indictment pleaded "not guilty" and a jury having been empanelled by the Provost Marshal to wit Thomas Hayes, George Thomas, George Anderson, Dominique Long, Francis Laudat and Edward B Preston and having made choice of Thomas Hayes for their foreman were duly sworn, and the evidence adduced in support of the prosecution as well as on behalf of the prisoner having been fully heard, pronounced by the foreman that the prisoner is "guilty" whereupon the court proceed to pass on him the sentence of the law by ordering him to be taken from whence he came and from thence to the usual place of execution there *to be hung by the neck until he be dead* whence His Excellency the Governor shall deem fit and his fees charged to the Colony. (CO 71/51)

10 OCTOBER 1814

By now, Ainslie had become ever more confident. Requesting the House of Assembly to attend Government House, he delivered this speech in which he commented on the deaths of "the supreme head" Jacko and other chiefs, and said that the island was now "almost free from those sanguinary marauders".

I congratulate the House on the return to their masters and habits of industry of so many Maroons, the interior of which not long since they had entire possession, being almost free from those sanguinary marauders. The supreme head as well as the principal chiefs have been killed with arms in their hands, and the colony enjoys a security which it has not known for a long series of years. Justice has been appeased by the sacrifice of eight or 10 lives at the place of execution, a necessity always to be deplored, but in this instance unavoidable when we consider that this daring Banditti was so formidable at the commencement of the year - as to concern the senior member of His Majesty's Council to seek refuge in town with his family, and a party of regular troops to protect his property although only half a mile distant. It is still fresh in the recollection of every person that a short time previous to my assuming the government a body of 20 armed Maroons entered this town, the capital of this island, and after robbing a house in one of the principal streets to the amount of 600 dollars in provisions so then retired unmolested. The expense of the establishment [of the Rangers] has no doubt been great but a considerable reduction may take place at the beginning of the year and although a few Maroons headed by the murderous Noel, are still at large, yet from the means employed only a very short time can elapse until he pays the forfeit of his guilty life.[27]

18 NOVEMBER 1814

Ainslie laid before the House of Assembly a memorandum from Captain Savarin naming the Ranger who killed Jacko and asking for his freedom

In the month of July last John LeVilloux, a private or corporal in the Ranger Corps killed Jacko, the head or principal chief of the Maroons, while this Jacko was in the act of firing at him. I beg leave to request His Excellency's recommendation to the House of Assembly for the freedom of the said John LeVilloux.[28]

22 NOVEMBER 1814

By the time Ainslie left Dominica for England on 22 November - at the request of the Colonial Office (see page 116) - his uncompromising attacks on the Maroons and their supporters on the estates appeared to have brought victory to the planters and their supporters. However, William Bremner remained cautious and commented in his memoirs that the Rangers should be maintained to prevent a return of "so dangerous an evil".

> A few weeks after Gov A's departure, Noel was shot by a party of Rangers and about the same time Apollo surrendered. Louis Moco, the only remaining chief of any name, soon after shared the fate of Noel; and before the end of the year 1814 the numbers who had surrendered, must have pretty well thinned the ranks of the Maroons. It was indeed considered that at this period their force was so effectually broken, that the number of the Rangers might be diminished to save expense to the colony, which indeed during this warfare had been immense, but it was very properly determined to keep up a part of that useful establishment as a permanent corps to prevent the recurrence of so dangerous an evil. (WB, p208)

10 DECEMBER 1814

This is the report that appeared in England on the death of Noel. With his killing, by a Loyal Dominica Ranger, the last notable chief was dead, and by the end of 1814 the Second Maroon War was over.

> We learn from Dominica, on the 10th of December, that the head of the infamous runaway Chief Noel was brought into that town [Roseau], by the Colonial Rangers. He was surprised alone on Tuesday last, near the former runaway camp, in the heights of Layon [sic], by a party who were on the alert. The guide was the first who perceived him, and immediately gave chase, making at the same time a signal to the party, who by a prompt movement surrounded him, and cut off his retreat into the thickets: he then attempted to make a resistance by drawing a long knife or cutlass he constantly wore, when the guide in self-defence levelled his musket and shot him. This miscreant was the person who perpetrated the murder of Mr McFarlane, and he was found clothed in the uniform jacket of his

unfortunate victim: it was brought to town with his head, which was ordered to be stuck on a pole at the other side of the river, as a salutary warning and example to others.[29]

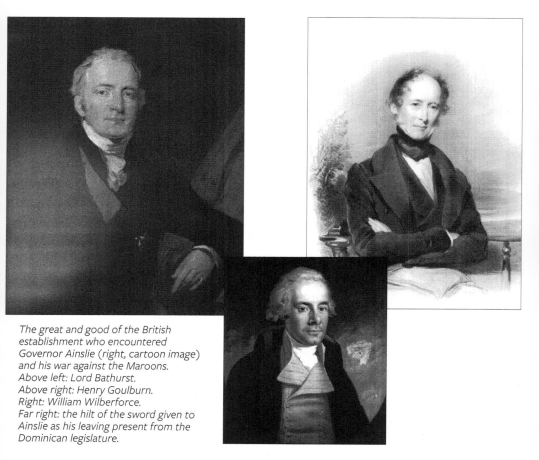

The great and good of the British establishment who encountered Governor Ainslie (right, cartoon image) and his war against the Maroons.
Above left: Lord Bathurst.
Above right: Henry Goulburn.
Right: William Wilberforce.
Far right: the hilt of the sword given to Ainslie as his leaving present from the Dominican legislature.

1814
A governor's defence

The news of Governor Ainslie's proclamations and policies towards the Maroons of Dominica was first reported in the English papers in January 1814. This alerted the British government to what was happening in its turbulent colony, and prompted Lord Bathurst, Ainslie's boss and Secretary of State for War and the Colonies, and his deputy, Henry Goulburn, to send letters to Ainslie asking him for an explanation. In response, Ainslie tried to describe the conditions in Dominica where, he said, the Maroons had created an "imperium in imperio" (a state within a state). But Bathurst was not convinced and requested that Ainslie return to London. Bathurst was a conciliatory and equable man and an abolitionist. He also believed that the interests of the British Empire were best served by curtailing the power of local governors and governments. Bathurst's patience with Ainslie would eventually run out.

In Dominica, with Maroon arrests, trials and executions intensifying through the first part of 1814 (see page 36-107), Ainslie's reputation as a robust defender of the status quo shone ever more brightly. The planters, merchants, the Church of all denominations and numbers of "people of colour" rallied to his defence praising his unequivocal attack on Maroon power.

Even so, Ainslie had to obey the Colonial Office in London, and he left Dominica for England in November 1814 with 200 guineas in his pocket to buy himself a sword from one of London's leading goldsmiths; it was a leaving present from his grateful legislature.

8 JANUARY 1814

The Royal Cornwall Gazette, Falmouth Packet and Plymouth Journal published a report about Ainslie's proclamation of 3 October 1813. This was probably the moment when the British establishment became aware of events in Dominica.

> A Proclamation issued at Dominica, by Governor Ainslie, after reciting that the detachments of troops, latterly sent in to the woods, had discovered traces of several runaway camps, and stating that His Excellency is still desirous of affording to those misguided slaves an opportunity of returning to their duty, offers an amnesty to all who shall surrender themselves, before the 24th of October, after which period they are to be treated with the utmost rigour of military execution, and put to the bayonet, without exception of age or sex.[1]

10 FEBRUARY 1814

The first official reaction from the British government about Ainslie's policies in Dominica came from Henry Goulburn, the Under-Secretary of State for War and the Colonies. Goulburn, who was well regarded by Bathurst for his diligence and efficiency, had inherited a plantation in Jamaica through his father but supported the gradual abolition of slavery. In this short - and measured - letter to Ainslie, Goulburn asked him to clarify the news that had reached England of Ainslie's proclamations. London wanted to know the facts.

> I have the honour of enclosing a copy of a paragraph which has appeared in many of the London newspapers. You must not suppose that I am induced to do it from any belief that the Proclamation alluded to in it has been issued, still less that it has been acted upon. The real ground of my troubling you on the subject is an anxiety to have it in my power to meet any observations which may be made on the subject in the House of Commons by a contradiction from authority and, as a paragraph in a newspaper cannot be made the subject of official correspondence, I have therefore taken the liberty of requesting by a private letter that you would give me any information in your power respecting the transaction to which the paragraph relates. (CO 72/10)

25 FEBRUARY 1814

Before Goulburn's letter to Ainslie of 10 February could arrive in Dominica, Ainslie made his fourth - and even more ferocious - proclamation concerning the Maroons. He reported on the progress of his subjugation of the Maroons, offered rewards for bringing in a chief, and made another threat telling the Maroons that unless they surrendered there would be no mercy. This proclamation ended with the sentence: "The Rangers have orders to take no prisoners but to put to death men, women, and children without exception." The Liverpool Mercury in England later reported that the proclamation was "abhorrent to our feelings as Englishmen and as friends of humanity. We are unable to imagine circumstances sufficiently dreadful to authorise such orders."[2]

> Whereas the camps of Jacko, Noel, Macho, Apollo, Diano and Sambo in the Layou District and those of the Elephant, and six others in the quarter of Couliabonne and on the River Claire have been utterly destroyed, the Chief Elephant[3] hanged and his head stuck up in Roseau and the Dominica Rangers stationed permanently in the woods for the purpose of harassing and pursuing to death such runaways as still keep out. Willing, however, to show mercy to those whom ignorance of my intention prevents returning to their masters, I, by this my proclamation, do declare that I will fully pardon all those who surrender themselves either to the commissioners of parishes, to their masters, or who appear at Government House Roseau before Monday the 21st day of March with the exception of the chief of the camp, and such as have committed murder and I do hereby offer besides a free pardon, 20 Joes reward to any runaway or runaways for every chief they bring to me and three Joes for each murderer; and thereby declare to the Maroons who are still in the woods that the Rangers have orders to take no prisoners but to put to death men, women, and children without exception. (CO 71/49)

26 FEBRUARY 1814

As well as men, the fight against the Maroons required arms. In this letter to Bathurst, Ainslie asked for arms - saying that the last time they had been supplied to Dominica was in 1789. He compared finding a way through Dominica's interior, the Maroons' stronghold, as being "almost as fatiguing" as climbing a Swiss mountain. At this time, Britain's military might was still preoccupied with fighting Napoleon in Europe and the United States in north America.

> I beg leave to call your Lordship's attention, once more, to the state of the Militia of this colony, where important services against the runaway Negroes, are much impeded, by the state of their arms, and accoutrements... I need not state, the total inability of the colony, in its present distressed situation to supply the deficiency. I begin to remark that the lighter the arms are, the better for the woods service, which is almost as fatiguing as that of the Chasseral[4] mountain in Switzerland, the places of retreat of the Maroons, being in a country, broken in the most singular manner and composed of wooded precipices; *fusils* are the only arms calculated for this country. Total required: 300 of each of musquets, ramrods, bayonets, slings, pouches, belts, bayonet belts, scabbards. (CO 71/49)

21 MARCH 1814

It is possible that this long and impassioned letter from Ainslie to Bathurst was a response to Henry Goulburn's request for an explanation of his conduct. In it, he explained in forthright terms the serious threat posed by the Maroons. He described the Maroons as an "imperium in imperio" (a state within a state) - a clear acknowledgment that the Maroons had developed an organised military, social and economic order with considerable capabilities in their forest fastnesses.

... People ignorant of the state of Dominica, erroneously believe, that the runaways are slaves, who to avoid punishment for some venial or menial offence, from a harsh master, run to the woods for a short time and then return to their duty, a few unfortunate, persecuted, isolated beings, without concert, whose only inheritance is slavery whose condition demands our pity... No misapprehension, Sir, can be greater. They are a Banditti under government of a chief, sub chiefs and captains, inhabiting a country difficult beyond description, having regular outposts/or camps as they are called, in advance of the Grand cantonment where the chief resides, with provision grounds cleared for miles; this "imperium in imperio" has been established above 30 years.

It is the practice of these people to increase their number, by enticing from their masters well-disposed Negroes, by means of [word missing] in which unfortunately they succeed too well, to the great loss of the planters, of whom a few months ago one advertised his estate for sale, in the Gazette as "his slaves had all run to the woods"!

Neither are their depredation on property, confined to this, they attacked and rob houses and estates to which the last [word missing] fugitives belonged, who are their guides, of which the following is a daring instance. A short time previous to my arrival, the cellar of a house on the market place of Roseau the chief town, was broken into, during the night, by a party of three miscreants, headed by the sub-chief Elephant who had run away from the unfortunate owners of the cellar, and carried off a considerable quantity of Madeira, and salted provisions undisturbed!

There are many instances of entire "gangs" of slaves, throwing off their allegiance to their masters, retiring to the woods and remaining until an overseer, whom they disliked, because he had ventured to inflict a well-merited punishment, was removed. Threats of murder and flames were conveyed to two very respectable proprietors of estates, both captains of Militia, and one, my deputy in his parish, from this same Elephant, who a few nights after, before he could put his threat in execution, was shot at the head of a party, in broad daylight, attacking for the avowed purpose of murder, the house of a small planter, which, during the absence of the owner, they had plundered of everything two days before. I have been obliged to furnish ammunitions to many of the poorer planters, not to attack but to defend their lives from these outlaws!

The evil had arrived at the most alarming magnitude, the slave population seemed animated by the unquiet spirit, which exploded, and founded a black government in St Domingo, the high tone of the French people of colour, had only been lowered, by administering the oath of allegiance to the King, to above 1000 of these (one of my first acts) an organised force (among whom some French deserters) in the interior in opposition to His Majesty's Government, plundering and murdering white and peaceable coloured inhabitants, life and property were equally insecure.

Such was the state of things, when I issued the proclamation, which has given rise to this correspondence, had I hesitated to adopt the most prompt and decided measures, I would have been wretchedly defunct in duty to His Majesty and unworthy of the station, I have the honour to fill.

From the moment I was issued with authority, this important object occupied my deepest attention; the season of the year precluding the practicability of certain operations, and wishing to mark my administration by clemency and its commencement, I offered to the Maroons a full pardon if they returned to their duty. I sent a slave, who, after surrendering, volunteered his services to the Grand Camp, with many copies of my proclamation, couched in language the fugitives could understand, this unfortunate man, Quashee the chief tried, and ordered to be shot, which was instantly executed. I set a price on the head of this barbarian, who, I understand, immediately offered 2000 dollars for mine.

The dry season affording a prospect of success I sent a strong detachment against the Maroons, but from the treachery of the guides, or the overwhelming hurricane of the 28th July, and almost equally destructive deluge of the 25th August, having totally changed the appearance of the country, they returned without having been able to reach their object.

This was the period when the proclamation in question was issued; no instance exists of any one being put to the bayonet. It was necessary to strike the Maroons with terror and success has justified my idea. Those put to death in the mountains, were shot running away, after invariably firing at their pursuers.

I transmit every public paper written by me, relative to these transactions, that you may see how invariably mercy has accompanied the steps [?] of justice; numbers are daily pardoned, even sub-chiefs, if not guilty of murder, and as the Rangers (a colonial corps of my organising) are vigorously pursuing those who still hold out, in their last retreat, powerfully aided by the desolation of their provision grounds, I trust that [this] country before next June will be completely cleared of those desperate bands of Maroons who for 30 years have set the law at defiance...

I shall be happy to hear that you have received this explanation the importance of which to me must be an apology for its length. (CO 71/49)

29 MARCH 1814

Before Bathurst could receive Ainslie's letter of 21 March, Bathurst wrote to the Governor expressing surprise that he had declared martial law and questioned the grounds for so doing.

> I confess that I learnt with some surprise that you had found it necessary to subject the colony to martial law, and though I am ready to admit that such a measure may be in some cases necessary yet I cannot sanction it without a more detailed statement of the causes which in your opinion justified such a proceeding. The mere fact of the increase of runaway slaves is certainly not an adequate ground for suspending the ordinary course of law nor do I consider that any advantage can have been derived from this measure either as to the detection or punishment of person guilty of offices which did not previously exist. (CO 72/10)

In the same letter, Lord Bathurst added a cryptic comment regarding a request from Ainslie that his brother be offered the job of Provost Marshal to replace James Laing whom Ainslie had described to Bathurst as being old and in England recovering from an accident. Bathurst wrote:

> ... Mr Laing whom you suppose to be on the point of death is fully able to retain his office of Provost Marshal. It is consequently unnecessary to advise to your recommendation of your brother... (CO 72/10)

23 APRIL 1814

This letter from Lord Bathurst to Ainslie was the strongest in tone yet: he demanded that Ainslie return to England to explain himself in view not only of the proclamations but of the declaration of martial law which had first taken place in January. Bathurst wanted to know what had happened and why.

> ... when I couple this intelligence with that which has already reached me of your having issued a proclamation of an outrageous nature (upon which my under secretary has sometime since received information) and of your having proclaimed martial law in the island, I am compelled to give more credit to the subsequent proceedings than I should otherwise have done, and as I look in vain to your correspondence for any information as to the measures which you might have had in contemplation I am under the necessity of signifying to you the pleasure of His Royal Highness the Prince Regent that you should take the first opportunity of returning home and giving a personal explanation of the measures which you have adopted, and of the motives which have led to their adoption. (CO 72/10)

25 APRIL 1814

With London now aware of Ainslie's policies, the situation in Dominica was raised in the House of Commons by Sir Henry Mildmay, better known as the seducer of Lady Rosebery, the wife of the fourth Earl of Rosebery. Mildmay asked Henry Goulburn (representing Lord Bathurst in the House of Commons) what the government knew about Ainslie's proclamation. Goulburn replied that he knew about it and had written to Ainslie but had yet to receive an answer.

> ... as soon as the proclamation appeared in the newspapers, it was submitted to Lord Bathurst; and a letter was sent to the West Indies, directing that a copy of it and any other document might be transmitted to England.[5]

10 JUNE 1814

While political pressure on Ainslie increased in London, his supporters in Dominica were quick to come to his defence. A number of affadavits were procured from grateful planters who, in six months, had seen the island returned to, as they saw it, relative tranquillity. This statement by James Labadie, planter and captain in the Royal St George's Regiment of Militia, for example, expressed the belief that since the declaration of martial law the "Negroes are reduced to complete order and rejection". He also discussed - as did others - the activities of Chief Elephant who had been active in the south of the island until he was shot by a planter. Labadie claimed that Elephant had threatened to:

> ...have his head and set fire to his father's estate in revenge, and... thinks that Elephant would certainly have endeavoured to put his threat into execution had he not been fortunately shot by Mr Gabriel Beauchamp whose house he attacked in the open day accompanied by several of his followers with the determination of murdering the said Beauchamp. Deponent further adds that had martial law not been declared and the subsequent measures taken that he verily believes the island would have been in a state of rebellion from the intercourse held between the Maroons and the slaves on the estate... since declaration of martial law that the Negroes are reduced to complete order and dejection... (CO 71/49)

Thomas Ferguson of Berricoa estate provided more information about Elephant.

> That your declarant was one of the Militia of this quarter who made the first incursion to the heights of the interior in an attack on Elephant's camp that the armed forces attacking was resisted by a volley of 15 to 20 gun shots that the said camp contained 35 or 40 Maroons and that only two infants were made captive by the assailants owing to the fortified and advantageous situation of said camp at that time.
>
> That from the deposition of some runaways who surrendered after the capture of said camp ... declared that the persons of Captain Labadie and Hiriart were designated for massacre and their properties marked out to be the first objects of arson and pillage. (CO 71/49)

Christopher Hiriart said that Elephant had declared his intention to "have my head". He also mentioned the presence of white deserters in the camp.

> ... there were 15 muskets in the camp and two white deserters who had instructed the runaways in the use of muskets drilling them every day which last fact has been proved the deserters having been taken and

punished by a general court martial ordered from headquarters [in] Barbados one with death the other very severe flogging and that I do really believe that the conduct of His Excellency the Governor has been the saving of the colony. (CO 71/49)

20 JUNE 1814

Boosted by such support, Ainslie sent a letter to Bathurst telling him that it was his "public duty" to finish his mission before returning to England.

21 JUNE 1814

Now that Bathurst's letter instructing Ainslie to return to England had arrived in Dominica, Ainslie had to convey the news to the Dominica legislature.

The Governor informs the Honourable House of Assembly that his Royal Highness the Prince Regent has signified his pleasure, through Earl Bathurst, Secretary of State for War and the Colonies, that he should return to Europe, to give some explanation relative to the operations carried on against the Maroons. George R. Ainslie, Governor.[6]

The Assembly replied by expressing their sorrow at the Governor's recall. They praised the measures he had pursued against the Maroons, and hoped for his speedy return. Support also came from 162 members of the white population who expressed their gratitude to the Governor in this statement. The letter was signed by the Anglican rector, the Revd HCC Newman, a known admirer of Ainslie, who later organised the publication of a booklet, printed in London, collating the sentiments of Ainslie supporters.[7]

We, the planters, merchants, and inhabitants of the island of Dominica, penetrated with a just sense of the important services which your Excellency has rendered generally to the inhabitants of this colony, and more particularly to the planters and owners of slaves, by your judicious and salutary measures for the suppression of a most alarming and dangerous rebellion among the Maroons, that has for a long series of years existed, and was daily increasing in number, force, and audacity, to

> the great terror and annoyance of the community, feel it an act of justice and a debt of gratitude due to your Excellency, to bear our unqualified testimony to your meritorious and well-timed exertions on this very serious and critical occasion.
>
> ... It is with regret we learn your Excellency's intended departure, particularly when we contemplate the possible consequences of your leaving the colony at this critical juncture; and our most earnest desire is, that your Excellency could be induced to remain among us until such time as the object, so nearly brought to a termination, shall be finally accomplished. Should you, however, Sir, have reasons for deciding otherwise (an event which we shall deeply regret), accept our best wishes for your health and happiness, and for your Excellency's speedy return to your government.
>
> HCC Newman, rector of the Parish of St George, Chairman.[8]

On the same day, 165 "people of colour" (the "most respectable of them"[9]) also rallied to Ainslie's cause. Such letters were most likely to have been composed by Newman himself.

> We, his Majesty's dutiful and loyal subjects, the inhabitants of colour of this island, having heard of your Excellency's premature departure, beg leave to offer our sincere acknowledgements and grateful thanks for your Excellency's timely and judicious measures taken in suppressing the late rebellion among the runaway slaves of this island, and we say in almost extirpating them from the woods, where they so long inhabited, and which rendered our lives and properties in perpetual danger, until the wise steps adopted by your Excellency had restored peace and tranquillity to every individual in this community; under these circumstances we cannot but regret your Excellency's departure... (CO 71/49)

12 JULY 1814

The events in Dominica and Ainslie's role there had stirred interest in England about his earlier behaviour as Lieutenant-Governor in Grenada where Mitchel, a free man of colour, had been flogged on Ainslie's orders. On the day that Jacko was killed in

Dominica (see p101), the abolitionist William Wilberforce presented the House of Commons with a petition from Mitchel.

> A petition was also presented to the House on the 12 July by Mr Wilberforce from a free man of colour, named Mitchel, at Grenada, complaining that, after he had obeyed the order of the Governor (Ainslie) by coming in, with other men of colour, within twenty-four hours after proclamation and taken the oaths of allegiance to his Majesty, he was afterwards taken by order of the Governor from his hut, where he was peaceably employed, by a military guard, brought to the public parade, and ordered by the Governor, who would not hear any remonstrance, nor assign any reason for his conduct, to be flogged by a country driver with 20 lashes upon his bare back, and then imprisoned until he was ordered to be sent out of the island; and praying such interference as the House in its wisdom should thing meet for his redress - Ordered to lie on the table.[10]

16 JULY 1814

Ainslie reported to Bathurst that Jacko had been shot but that Noel, "the wanton murderer of a white man", remained at large. He also claimed that "since I commenced operations against the Maroons, in January last, I can hear of no instance of a single Negro deserting from his master."

> Jacko, the Supreme Chief who titled himself "governor of the woods", he was shot in the act of levelling at the Sergeant Major of the Colonial Rangers. He possessed great influence over the other camps, who acknowledge his supreme power, and I think his death's a great circumstance. I mean to shed no more blood, except that of a chief named Noel, the wanton murderer of a white man, a Mr McFarlane, who was put to death by him while sheltering in his house. It may appear worthy of remark that since I commenced operations against the Maroons in January last, I can hear of no instance of a single Negro deserting from his master.
>
> NB: Jacko had been in the woods for 46 years in hostility to his Majesty's Government. (CO 71/49)

17 JULY 1814

Ainslie wrote to Bathurst mentioning that he had shown mercy to a young pregnant woman and her child. He appeared to be trying to gain Bathurst's approval for what he calls "this trifling grant".

> Among the prisoners taken in the woods was a young woman far advanced in pregnancy, with a miserable young child in her hand, having been born in the woods of unknown parents, she had no owner or person to claim her. I therefore, instead of selling, gave her to a person, who has promised to treat her and her other children well, and has been at the [illegible word] of her confinement, which happened almost immediately after her arrival in town. I hope, I have not in this, exceeded my powers, and that your Lordship will approve of this trifling grant in favour of a very deserving person. (CO 71/49)

29 AUGUST 1814

Ainslie dissolved the elected House of Assembly. It had been much divided and proved less supportive of Ainslie than the Council, whose members were appointees of the Governor. The House of Assembly was elected from a very restricted number of enfranchised people.

> Whereas I judged it necessary to call together the House of Assembly for the dispatch of public business of the colony, and as the majority of that house have, in times of unexampled distress, shown themselves totally negligent of the interest of their constituents; inasmuch as during the course of 13 months only two bills have been offered for my sanction, one of which has been rejected, it is my will and pleasure that the house be dissolved, to give the country an opportunity of showing their sense of the services of their representatives; and the house is hereby dissolved accordingly. Given under my hand and seal-at-arms, at Roseau, the 29th day of August, 1814, and 54th year of His Majesty's reign.[11]

8 SEPTEMBER 1814

Bathurst reminded Ainslie that if he had not done so already he should leave

Dominica in some haste - in obedience to his earlier instructions.

> I am persuaded that nothing short of the strong conviction you must have felt that your presence at Dominica was at the time indispensably necessary could have induced you to hesitate respecting the course you had to adopt upon the receipt of my dispatch of the 23 April last.
>
> I am satisfied however that the circumstances which gave rise to the instructions contained in that dispatch will render you anxious to avail yourself of the earliest opportunity of returning to this country in obedience thereto, in case you should not already have taken your departure from Dominica, which under every view of the subject is more to be expected. (CO 72/10)

20 OCTOBER 1814

Three months after Ainslie received his instructions to return to England, he wrote this short letter to Bathurst announcing his plans. Ainslie had also been thwarted by a lack of shipping - Britain was then engaged in the 1812 war with the United States - to take him back across the Atlantic.

> I have received your Lordship's despatch of the 8th September and beg to acquaint you that I shall leave this colony for Europe on the 8 November. (CO 71/49)

3 NOVEMBER 1814

Just before he left Dominica, Ainslie was still receiving endorsements from his supporters in respect of his proclamations. Here, Captain Savarin, the leader of the Loyal Dominica Rangers, writes in Ainslie's defence.

> I do hereby certify and declare on my honour, that I never received order from His Excellency Governor Ainslie to put to death any runaways, either men, women or children as stated in His Excellency's proclamation. And that I never gave any such order to the officers and men under my command; the contrary was the fact; as on all occasions every humanity consistent with our own safety, when engaged in the

mountains with them, has been shown to these poor deluded wretches, as well by His Excellency as myself. That on no occasion was a child ever killed or even hurt - on the contrary there were many instances when children and even women were carried out of the woods and mountains on the Rangers' back. (CO 71/49)

11 NOVEMBER 1814

The House of Assembly had proposed a payment of £1000 in gratitude for Ainslie's efforts, of which 200 guineas was for the purchase of a sword with the word "extinction" to be part of the inscription relating to Ainslie's triumph over the Maroons. However, the Board of the Council disagreed with the use of the word "extinction" because the colony was still in danger from the "desperadoes" in the forest. Here are the Council's comments on the choice of words.

"[The Board] willingly acknowledge that much has been done towards the suppression of the Renegades. It is nevertheless true, that a large proportion of those who have either been taken or have voluntarily delivered themselves up, consist of women and children, and that a very small comparative number of adult males have yet been either apprehended or surrendered while therefore two such notoriously desperate characters as Noel and Apollo continue to head a body of runaways in the woods whose numbers it is to be feared are yet considerable and who may reasonably be deposed from their determined resistance to submission to consist of desperadoes like their leaders [while] such a formidable body still exists and continues to elude all the vigilance and defie all the exertions of the Rangers, the Board can never consent to sanction a declaration that those hordes are extinguished or that the colony is yet placed in anything like a state of complete safety from so dangerous and intestine enemy.

18 NOVEMBER 1814

A war of words then ensued. The House of Assembly hit back by accusing the Council of "malicious, insidious and false insinuation" in claiming that most of the Maroons who surrendered were women and children. In the end, the Council got its way. Ainslie's leaving present was inscribed "in testimony of his meritorious conduct in the reduction of the Maroons, in the year 1814". It was signed by Archibald Gloster, President, and William Anderson, Speaker. The minutes of the House of Assembly record that Ainslie thanked the two houses for:

> ... the handsome manner in which they have conferred upon him a sword for what they have been pleased to term services which are however infinitely overrated.

22 NOVEMBER 1814

Ainslie left Dominica on 22 November for England after a stay in Dominica of one and a half years during which he won many admirers in the parlours, plantation houses, merchants' homes and rum shops of the island but few elsewhere. Ainslie may have left Dominica, but on his return to England at the beginning of 1815 he continued to defend his track record against those who had set themselves against the colonial regime and its representatives.

Right: the chamber of the House of Commons at the beginning of the 19th century. The execution of Quashie of Woodford Hill was discussed there in June 1815. Below: The market place in Roseau, where Quashie and others were executed.

1815
Maroons defeated, Ainslie sacked

By 1815 the Maroons had been crushed but Governor Ainslie, too, was being called to account. Summoned back to London from Dominica, Ainslie spent much of that year justifying his conduct to Lord Bathurst at the Colonial Office and defining himself as the "saviour of the island". In a volley of letters in a sloping, scratchy hand, the Governor defended his conduct in Dominica - and his character: "From several circumstances I am led to believe that your Lordship supposed me of an irritable temper in such cases one's own opinion has little weight, but I can confidently appeal to a very numerous list of acquaintances, that I am far from being considered either a passionate or ill-natured man."[1]

Ainslie lobbied to return to Dominica to finish what he considered to be unfinished business, but in June 1815, his behaviour in both Grenada and Dominica was debated in the House of Commons where the question of the legality of the execution of Quashie from Woodford Hill was raised; William Wilberforce also became briefly involved when he was sent a letter purporting to come from a J. Clapham of Roseau accusing Ainslie for ordering the flogging of four Black soldiers without trial. Ainslie's critics requested that he should not be allowed to return to Dominica until matters of legality and morality had been investigated, and the British government agreed.

In Dominica, the business of the colony rested with Benjamin Lucas, the caretaker head of the island's administration. Lord Bathurst repeatedly asked him to send the minutes of the trials and a complete list of the Maroons who had been killed or had surrendered. The Colonial Office would not have routinely requested such documents - but then this was not a normal situation. Lucas was forced to apologise for the delay blaming Ainslie and Glanville, the Attorney General. Eventually he managed to put them on a boat bound for London. At the end of the year, Bathurst told Ainslie that he would not be returning to Dominica. Ainslie - but not the system - had been found unfit for purpose.

3 JANUARY 1815

Benjamin Lucas, now standing in for Ainslie as the most senior member of the legislature, sent a message to the two legislative houses informing them that the Dominica Rangers should be reduced but only gradually so that the Maroons would not regroup. He stated that the cost of the Rangers up to 24 December 1814 had been £10,504 12 shillings and 11 pence (approx EC$2.5m or £620,000 in today's money) - and that this sum omitted costs of arms, clothing and accoutrement ordered from England. He admitted that the cost had been high. He also announced the death of Chief Noel, the last Maroon chief to be killed.

> I am, however, happy to congratulate you on a further reduction of the numbers of the runaways, by the surrender of several of them, principally men, but more particularly on the destruction of that desperate chief and murderer Noel, who refused to surrender to a detachment of the Rangers sent in pursuit of him and by whom he was shot.[2]

JANUARY 1815 [UNDATED]

Arriving back in England, Governor Ainslie installed himself in London and in rural Lincolnshire, the home of his wife's family. Almost immediately, he wrote to Lord Bathurst from his London address at 18 Bury Street, asking for a brief meeting that would take no more than five minutes as "Mr Wilberforce says 'he had no intention of instituting any proceeding respecting me'."[3] Most probably this reference to William Wilberforce related to the flogging in Grenada of Mitchel, the free man of colour whose petition Wilberforce had placed before the British parliament. *(see p121)*

19 MARCH 1815

In a letter from Fulbeck in Lincolnshire to Bathurst, Ainslie complained about his health, in particular his liver (he was known to be an intemperate drinker) but offered to return to Dominica "at a moment's notice".

> ... I shall be ready at a moment's notice to return to my government of Dominica should the situation of public affairs render this immediately necessary, although the affliction of my liver, and my impaired sight make

me desirous of prolonging my stay in England, till the first week in May. (CO 71/50)

4 APRIL 1815

Ainslie's correspondence with the Colonial Office continued. In this letter to Henry Goulburn, Under Secretary of State for War and the Colonies, he attacked Benjamin Lucas while boasting of his own achievements.

... I foresee a renewal of the political disorders (from the total incapacity of Mr Lucas to administer any government) which I had succeeded in tranquillising, and I therefore am anxious to return forthwith, and I request you will have the goodness to acquaint my Lord Bathurst with my intention, to which I trust [he] has no objection...

I believe there are not 20 runaways or Maroons. The murderer of Mr McFarlane[4], whom I excepted from mercy on that account, has been killed. Apollo, the remaining one, has been pardoned by my order and now a trusty guide in the Colonial Rangers. I consider the security of the island complete which has been repeatedly attempted by former governors, at a great expense of blood, I have succeeded in restoring 542 slaves to their master and habits of industry with the loss in all of 22 lives. (CO 71/50)

6 APRIL 1815

Two days later, Ainslie wrote a private letter to Goulburn, with a further attack on Benjamin Lucas calling him an "imbecile". He asked Goulburn to say "two words by return if you can" to allow his return to Dominica. (CO 71/50)

19 APRIL 1815

Meanwhile, in Dominica, the House of Assembly began to reward slaves who had served with the Rangers. It resolved that Sergeant Gardier Coipel should be paid £3 6 shillings a month "for the loss of his arm by a gun shot wound from Noel a runaway while actually serving with the Ranger Corps" and £3 12 shillings a month when he left the Corps. The government also announced freedom for the two Rangers who had killed Chiefs Noel, Louis Moco and Jacko.

The following Rangers be manumitted at the expense of the colony that remain on the Corps or employed in any other duty for the benefit of the colony. viz: Joe Gibbon for killing Noel, John LeVilloux for killing Louis Mocco [sic] and Jacco [sic], the supreme chief of the runaways, and that the treasurer be directed to pay the owners of the said slaves their estimated value on their joining the Ranger Corps and that a certified copy of a joint resolution of the legislature of this effect to be lodged with the treasurer which will be deemed a sufficient proof of freedom... [5]

7 MAY 1815

... that the sum of £66 each to be paid to the Ranger Corps for killing Old Jacko, Quashy, Noel and Louis Moco.[6]

11 MAY 1815

In England, Ainslie found himself at the centre of another possible investigation when William Wilberforce received a letter from a "J. Clapham" in Dominica. It appeared that Wilberforce, who knew of Ainslie's reputation in Grenada, had heard that Ainslie was due to return to Dominica so he decided to pass the letter on to his old acquaintance Lord Bathurst whom he addresses (in this letter marked "private") as "My dear Lord B". The "enclosed" that Wilberforce referred to was a letter that Ainslie claimed to be a forgery: it accused Ainslie of having had Black soldiers flogged without trial for having arrived late while escorting him on a tour of the island.

My dear Lord B
Ever since I received the enclosed which was a very few days ago, I have been doubting whether I ought or ought not to transmit it to you. But not knowing who Mr Clapham is I paused that I might inquire and afterwards act as might be proper. But hearing that Gen Ainslie was going out again I feel it my duty to send you the [?] letter. The Duke of Gloucester has received a similar one - and entre nous, there are several members of both houses who are acquainted both with this case and Mitchel's. I could call instead of writing but for being engaged at a public meeting all day. (CO 71/50)

MAY 1815 [UNDATED]

An undated and un-authored note (perhaps originating in the Colonial Office) documented Ainslie's request for information about the complaints that had been made against him; it also named those whom Ainslie believed were behind the letter from "J. Clapham".

> Major General Ainslie begs Mr Goulbourn to give him another cover, and to let him have Sir Sam Romilly's precise motion last night as he is quite at a loss to know the object it has in view, he wishes to know what other complaints are against him that he may give every explanation without delay. Mr Wilberforce has been good enough to send a copy of the letter signed "J. Clapham" to Mr George Ainslie who will almost stake his existence on the opinion that it is the joint production of President Lucas, his secretary Armatrading[7] and a man named Hayes who married the old woman Clapham's daughter. (CO 71/50)

13 MAY 1815

This letter from Goulburn to Ainslie referred to Lord Bathurst's surprise that Ainslie should be considering a return to Dominica before the matter of the allegedly forged letter had been investigated.

> I am directed by Lord Bathurst to transmit to you a copy of a letter which he received on the evening of the 11th inst purporting to be addressed to HRH the Duke of Gloucester, which his Lordship has thought it his duty to transmit for the consideration of his Royal Highness the Commander in Chief. As this letter, if really addressed to His Highness, must from its date have been received a considerable time since, Lord Bathurst concludes that its contents must have been made known to you before, and under this impression his Lordship cannot but express his surprise that you should have entertained the idea of returning to Dominica before the circumstances stated in it had undergone a complete investigation. (CO 72/10)

Ainslie continued to write to Goulburn begging him to let him know what complaints had been made against him. The tone of the letters became increasingly beseeching. He also pressed upon Goulburn affidavits from Dominica in his support. (CO 71/50)

27 MAY 1815

Ainslie wrote to Major General Sir Henry Torrens, military secretary to the Commander in Chief of the British forces, and described the circumstances around the flogging of the Pioneers (Black soldiers) as alluded to in the letter from the mysterious J. Clapham. Ainslie said the incident took place in May 1813 - one month after his arrival in Dominica - although the complaint was deliberately not made until February 1815 when he was no longer on the island. He also claimed that "after the most minute enquiry" the only person "of that name [Clapham] who has been known or who has resided in the island of Dominica died about 20 years ago".[8] *He went on to describe how members of the Pioneers had been instructed to accompany him - to carry baggage and to cover 10 miles a day - on a tour of the island to meet up with military officials. On the first three days they were late arriving, and on the fourth day they took 11 hours to cover six miles.*

> ... I was compelled in order to enforce obedience to just and reasonable orders to have recourse to that species of correction which I hoped would produce reform and would be attended with no inconvenience to the individuals.
>
> With this view I directed that 12 strokes should be given to each of the Pioneers on the outside of their ordinary dress, which consisted of thick blue woollen cloth trousers, and I particularly directed that the strokes should be so given, as not to inflict smart pain.

Ainslie defended his decision not to hold a court martial saying that it would have delayed proceedings. He argued that there had been no complaints - neither by the Pioneers nor by any officers - and that the punishment was not excessive. He did, however, admit that holding a court martial

> ... might have been more strictly within the line of military rule but it would have been attended with no advantage to the public service on which I was then engaged. (CO 71/50)

1 JUNE 1815

Ainslie's troubles were exacerbated by another complaint on a completely different subject. In this letter, Henry Goulburn referred to correspondence from Robert Aberdeen, owner of Woodford Hill estate, about the trial of Quashie and Mills (see page 90). The same subject would be raised the next day in the House of Commons. Goulbourn also requested the minutes of the courts martial of 1814.

> I am directed by Lord Bathurst to transmit to you the enclosed copy of a letter which has been received this day by his Lordship and to request that you will afford him every explanation in your power relative to the transaction to which it alludes. I am at the same time directed to enquire whether you have the means of furnishing his Lordship with the minutes of the proceedings of the several courts martial held by you for the trials of the Maroons and runaway slaves in the island of Dominica. (CO 72/11)

2 JUNE 1815

In a debate in the House of Commons, Robert "Bum" Gordon, MP for Wareham, proposed a motion that a committee be set up to investigate the conduct of Ainslie both in Grenada and in Dominica. Gordon, whose father and grandfather owned a plantation in Jamaica, supported the interests of the West Indian planters but was known for his independent thinking and belief that "the domination of the whites would be best maintained by kindness to the slaves".[8] In his speech, he also drew attention to a letter that he had received from Mr Aberdeen. According to Aberdeen, his manager had told him that a messenger from Governor Ainslie had arrived at his estate with a box containing Quashie's head. Mr Gordon reported that Mr Aberdeen was surprised that the Colonial Office would be considering sending Ainslie back to Dominica under these circumstances.

> Mr Gordon.
> ... A most respectable gentleman, Mr Aberdeen, a man of large property in the island [Dominica], had received a letter here in London from his manager, dated the 4th of last June, in which he stated, that information having been given to Governor Ainslie that two slaves were in communication with the runaways camp, and had sold them some

provisions, which, however, were not the property of their masters, he [Ainslie] ordered the writer, the manager in question, to have them arrested, and sent to him into the town. They were sent, but this person did not accompany them, because he was not aware that any violent proceedings were in contemplation; but in a few days afterwards a messenger arrived from the Governor, with a box upon his head, and a letter, saying, "I have executed one of the two slaves you sent me, after being tried by a court martial, and this is his head, which you are to place on a pole upon the estate!"—(Hear, hear!) The other slave was imprisoned, and afterwards shipped off the island.

The hon. gentleman said he had asked Mr Aberdeen, why, if he had received this letter so long ago, he had not taken some steps upon it before now; and he answered, that he had communicated it to the Secretary of State [Lord Bathurst], adding that he had no idea government would ever have thought of sending the general back to the island. On the whole, to say the least, Governor Ainslie had been guilty of such great indiscretion, that he appeared ignorant of the colonial laws, and was unfit to be a governor. All such persons ought to be of mild dispositions, and not given to passion.

The hon. gentleman then adverted to the condition of the slaves in our colonies, which was susceptible of great amelioration; and he called on those members who had so nobly exerted themselves in effecting the abolition of the trade, to reflect that much remained to be done. He had some hundreds of slaves under his own protection, and he felt that he should best perform his duty and consult his interest by considering how he could ameliorate their situation.[9]

In the same debate, Sir Robert Heron MP, defended Ainslie despite later (in his memoirs) describing him as "without judgment, his temper naturally too irritable, rendered more so by the habit of drinking continued in a hot climate had, certainly, been guilty of many great indiscretions."[10] In a long speech Heron discussed, among other things, the accusation made against Ainslie over the flogging of the four soldiers, his behaviour in Grenada over the flogging of Jean Mitchel, and his conduct in pursuing the Maroons in Dominica. He ended by supporting Ainslie over the conduct of Quashie's trial and describing his activities in Dominica as "highly meritorious".

> The honourable gentleman has told us a romantic story of a head in a box... the two men were condemned to death by a court martial; after a fair trial, they were fully convicted of supplying the insurgents with provisions and ammunition: instead of cruelty, the Governor showed great lenity in putting only one of them to death. When the head was severed from the body, the manner of its disposal does not seem very important; the fact however is, that it was sent to the place where the crime was committed (in a box) to be exposed on a pole; this practice was frequent, because it was found beneficial. By the means I have described, the Governor succeeded in putting an end to the war, and saved the colony....[11]

MP Sir Samuel Romilly, an abolitionist and law reformer, took a different position. In his speech, Romilly drew attention to the "prejudices against people of colour"[12] *held by West Indian planters, queried the justification of Ainslie's proclamation and, in his memoirs, argued that the attacks on the Maroons were a pretext for "getting a supply of fresh Negroes".*

> It did not appear that the island [Dominica] was in any such state as could justify the publishing of such a proclamation, even if it were merely meant as a threat... For myself, I very much suspect that this expedition against the wild Negroes, who have existed, I believe, in the mountains ever since the island became part of the British possessions (which was at the peace of 1763) was merely a pretext for extirpating (what certainly is a great inconvenience) the haunts of these people, to which all runaway Negroes may resort as to an asylum; and for getting a supply of fresh Negroes for the plantations of individuals, which cannot, since the abolition of the slave trade, be procured by any regular means.[13]

At the end of the debate, Henry Goulburn promised that Ainslie would not be allowed to return to Dominica until the matter concerning Jean Mitchel, which was being addressed by the British courts, had been settled. Gordon then agreed to withdraw his motion.

2 JUNE 1815

On the same day as the debate in the House of Commons, Ainslie replied to Goulburn defending the judicial process in the courts martial of Quashie and Mills and its aftermath.

> In answer to yours of yesterday's date I beg to state for the information of Lord Bathurst that Mills and Quashee[14] were convicted either by the civil power or a general court martial of holding intercourse with, and supplying the Maroons with arms, ammunition and salt, an article of the first necessity to them. Quashee was hanged and Mills was banished. It was of great importance to make an example of those who fostered the spirit of rebellion by supplying the Maroons with the means of hostility, which was carried on most extensively as well as with great secrecy, and to the difficulty of bringing guilt home may be ascribed the want of success which has attended all former attempts to subdue the Maroons.
>
> Mr Fraser, a member of the [Dominica] House of Assembly, a considerable landed proprietor himself and attorney of estates, was on the spot when the discovery of Quashee's guilt was made of which he apprised and begged me to have them both tried without delay and I can safely state that the detection of Mills and Quashee was a subject of congratulation in the island, in as much as it would cut off the resources the Maroons possessed of supplies... They both had a fair trial and Quashee confessed his guilt previous to his execution.
>
> The heads of notorious malefactors were usually applied for by the proprietors to have them placed on poles for the sake of example, for which purpose I sent Quashee's to Mr Denbow, the manager, the estate being three or four days' journey and heat of the climate not permitting me to keep the head above ground until I could get his answer.
>
> I cannot close this explanation without remarking that Mr Aberdeen seems to place more weight on the value of his slave than on the safety of

> the island which this man was sapping. I profess no means of furnishing his Lordship with the minutes of the court martial, which are I suppose preserved in the proper office in Dominica. I always read them over with attention and in more instances than one sent them back for revisal, which shows that no indecent hurry took place. I believe every culprit acknowledged his guilt to his religious adviser before execution. (CO 71/50)

7 JUNE 1815

In a further speech in the House of Commons, Sir Samuel Romilly commented that it was not legitimate to return to their owners slaves who had been in the forest for many years since it would be difficult to prove that ownership. A few days earlier Romilly had been at a meeting at which the registration of slaves in the West Indies was discussed; this was not, at this point, favoured by the British government although it was subsequently adopted. In his memoirs, Romilly wrote that he

> ... asked that there be laid before the House an account of the 615 persons of colour stated in the return of Governor Ainslie to have been restored to their owners, and many of them to have been from 10 to 35 years in the woods.[15]

9 JUNE 1815

A rambling letter from Ainslie (probably to Goulburn) stated that Mr Fraser, Aberdeen's attorney, was the one who instigated the trials of Quashee and Mills. Ainslie also claimed that the mystery J. Clapham, whom he now identified as Mistress Johanna Clapham, was illiterate.[16]

> Referring to my statement of 2 June inst relative to Mr Aberdeen's slaves Quashee and Milne [sic], I have now to add that Mr Fraser who requested me to send for these people, who (I believe) was present at the trial, who first investigated the case on the estate before he judged them fit subjects for trial, and who has often expressed his great satisfaction at the detention of these culprits, is attorney and agent for Mr Aberdeen, and most likely [illegible word] him very differently from his manager

(similar to farming man in England), on this subject which he himself had seen the operation of in all its stages. But this did not seem the purpose of Mr Aberdeen it was necessary that he should have an excuse to stay in England instead of going to Antigua, and to gain this object he ungenerously attempted the ruin of one who has saved his whole property from destruction, and who is known to him only in that light.

I trust that this complaint as well as the Black Pioneers (for I have on Sunday last, found proof, that even Mistress Johanna of Clapham never could write) will show Lord Bathurst the malevolent spirit which pervades the whole of these accusations, an unfortunate attendant on public men who conscientiously discharged the functions of their office. (CO 71/50)

15 JUNE 1815

In this letter to Benjamin Lucas in Dominica, Lord Bathurst - having failed to obtain the minutes of the trials from Ainslie - requested them from Lucas. He also asked for further information about the trial of Quashie and Mills whom he had heard were "unjustly and illegally condemned".

It being necessary with a view to certain inquiries now conducting in this country that I should be furnished with information respecting the proceedings against the Maroons and runaway Negroes brought to trial in Dominica whether before a court martial or the ordinary civil courts, I am to desire that you will transmit to me the minutes of the proceedings which took place upon their trials specifying distinctly the charge upon which each person was tried, the sentence passed upon him, and the mode in which that sentence was executed. And as it has been represented to me that two Negroes of the names of Quashy [sic] and Milne [sic], the property of Mr Aberdeen, were unjustly and illegally condemned, I have to direct the transmission of every further particular respecting these two persons which it may be in your power to furnish. (CO 72/11)

9 JULY 1815

In Sir Henry Torrens' reply to Ainslie about the flogging of the Pioneer soldiers, Ainslie escaped being formally investigated although he was clearly reprimanded: according to Torrens, His Royal Highness "is induced to recommend that the matter shall be passed over, with the expression of his disapprobation at the undue exercise of authority, which you most erroneously, and improperly, adopted, upon the occasion alluded to". However, Torrens went on to make a vigorous point that Black soldiers should be treated in the same manner as European soldiers.

> ... HRH has been further induced to this lenient consideration of the case in question from a conviction of your good intentions and a knowledge of your zeal for the service which, though it may lead you into error, can never, he is persuaded, find any origin in an improper motive. But he desires I will impress upon your mind, that when Negroes become soldiers in His Majesty's service, they are equally claimants with any part of the forces to the impartial protection of military law, and are immediately exempt from any arbitrary exercise of power usually practised towards their fellow countrymen in servitude. Not withstanding therefore the temporary inconvenience to which you may have been subjected by the misconduct of these people, during your tour in Dominica you had no more right to exercise a discretionary punishment upon them, than if they had been European soldiers, and HRH desires that your usual attention to the services may be afforded, towards a future circumspection towards such subjects. (CO 71/50)

19 JULY 1815

In an affadavit Alexander Fraser, Mr Aberdeen's attorney, said that he regretted that Mills was not also executed - as he was a "notorious old offender".[16]

21 JULY 1815

In this statement from L'Abbe John Joseph Piron, "curate of the Roman Catholics" and an Ainslie supporter, Piron described how he had visited condemned Maroons in jail before their execution, and that they had told him that they had not "paid attention and conformed to the several proclamations published by his Excellency Governor Ainslie":

> ... but that they were afraid of being killed by the chiefs of their camps who put to death every individual suspected of an intention to return to their masters - which had been actually practised in the camps on several Negroes whose hearts were torn out, and after being dried in the smoke of their fires, were exposed upon a pole at the entrance of the other camps. (CO 71/50)

25 JULY 1815

The affair surrounding Quashie rumbled on. This affadavit is from John Moody, a constable who had escorted Quashie and Mills from Woodford Hill to jail in Roseau.

> On his arrival there [Woodford Hill] he delivered the Marshal's letter to Mr Denbow, the manager who observed that it was too late to do anything that night. That in the morning Mr Denbow took him to the works of the estates and sent the driver to call Quashee and Mills before him. On their arrival, they were secured, and Mr Denbow sent to inform Mr Simpson, the Commissioner of the Quarter thereof, who came to Woodford Hill and conceiving that a rescue of the two Negroes would be attempted ordered a corporal and four privates of the company of Militia under his command to conduct them to Prince Rupert's [Bay], a distance of about 20 miles. Mr Denbow observed that Quashee was a vile scoundrel...
>
> Moody also said that when they arrived at Prince Rupert's, soldiers of the 6th regiment quartered there told him that a few days previous he [Quashee] had bought from the soldiers a large quantity of salt beef and pork and that he had often seen him in the garrison purchasing salt provision for which he always paid cash. (CO 71/50)

2 AUGUST 1815

The minutes of Dominica's Privy Council stated that Lord Bathurst had asked for information "regarding the conduct of the late Maroon war in Dominica, and I am to desire that you will by the earliest opportunity transmit to me the information required." The minutes also noted that Lucas was having trouble obtaining it.

> ... His Honor [Lucas] sent to Mr Bruce [Ainslie's secretary] to desire he would furnish him with such public documents as were in his possession relative to the runaways in order to enable his Honor to give Lord Bathurst the information required, that Mr Bruce instead of original papers sent what he called a general return of runaways which referred to other papers enclosed, being returns and extracts from the Marshal's books[17] and certificates from Captain Savarin, that these papers appearing to be incomplete and incorrect his Honor sent again to Mr Bruce for original papers which Mr Bruce has thought proper to refuse, that one of the papers sent by Mr Bruce purporting to be a return of runaways committed to gaol from 23 April 1813 to 19 May 1814 and signed Edward H Beech being incorrect and complete... Mr Beech has also thought proper to refuse to part with it out of his possession or to bring it himself to Government House alleging it to be a private document... (CO 71/50)

24 AUGUST 1815

Finally, Lucas was able to send Bathurst "The accounts of the slaves brought to trial as runaways, or for having harboured, supplied, or had intercourse with runaways, together with copies of the minutes of the proceedings of the courts martial and courts of special sessions held between the 10 May 1813, the date of Governor Ainslie's proclamation, and the 22 day of November 1814, the date of Ainslie's departure from this island." Having mentioned that the evidence was not in proper order, he went on to say:

> I have also the honour to enclose copies of three warrants[18] signed by Governor Ainslie for the execution of slaves, which are all that I can procure; Mr Beech, who acted some time as Provost Marshal, having informed me that he executed the sentences of courts martial without any warrants, considering the sentences themselves, when approved by the Governor, to be sufficient authority. (CO 71/50)

28 AUGUST 1815

A further letter was sent to Bathurst with an enclosure entitled "An account of runaway slaves killed, taken and surrendered between the 10th day of May 1813, the date of Governor Ainslie's proclamation, and the 22nd day of November 1814, the day of his departure from Dominica, distinguishing the sexes and the children; with the manner in which they have been disposed of." Lucas was not happy about the accuracy of the material but told Bathurst that it was all he could obtain.(CO 71/50)

The account was divided into five categories and contained the following information:

1. *Maroons killed. It included four chiefs: Elephant (7 February 1814), George Anderson, owner, killed by manager of Benbro estate; Moco George (20 April 1814), Mr Blondel, owner, killed by Loyal Dominica Rangers; Gabriel (30 April 1814), owner unknown, killed by Loyal Dominica Rangers; and Old Jacko (12 July 1814), Mr Beaubois, owner [Castle Comfort] killed by Loyal Dominica Rangers, called "the oldest chief". Total: 15 men and three women.*
2. *Runaway slaves taken by the Loyal Dominica Rangers, by the Militia or volunteers sent against the runaways, or by soldiers at signal posts etc or sent to jail as runaways, having been in camps or parties of runaways in the wood. Total: 109 men, 111 women and 68 children.*
3. *Runaway slaves surrendered to the Loyal Dominica Rangers. Total: six men, one woman.*
4. *Slaves taken up by managers of plantations, by constables in town, loitering about off the plantations to which they belong without passes; caught breaking canes, or pilfering in the neighbouring provision grounds, but who do not appear to have been in any camp, or to have joined any party of runaways. Total: 100 men, 48 women, five children.*
5. *Slaves, stated by Mr Bruce, the Governor's secretary, to have surrendered to the Governor, and pardoned by him, and restored to their owners. Total: 75 men, 31 women and five children.*

Total: 305 men, 194 women and 78 children.

Total: 577

In a further sentence, the document refers to those enslaved who may have returned to their owners who did not report them. "Captain Savarin believes they may amount to one hundred."[19]

5 SEPTEMBER 1815

In England, Ainslie continued to argue for his return to Dominica. He wrote to Goulburn to say "that the almost unanimous wish of all ranks and colours in the colony [was] for my speedy return", and that "petitions have been sent... which will at least show Mr Gordon and Sir Samuel Romilly that the people... have formed a different opinion as to my fitness to govern to that expressed by those gentlemen". In the same letter he also referred to the case regarding "Old Mrs Clapham" and also to the rights and wrongs of the trial of Quashie of Woodford Hill.

> Old Mrs Joanna Clapham denies all knowledge of the malicious letter to the Duke of Gloucester respecting the Black soldiers, His Highness has been therefore the dupe of some miscreants afraid to show themselves; a message to me would have saved his Highness' secretary and your office some trouble, it has opened the door to interminable complaints. The person who complained that Mr Aberdeen's slave Quashee was tried without his (the manager) being approached I now prove by affidavit to be false, as he Mr Denbow ... has declared that Quashee instead of being a well-disposed Negro as he called him to Mr Aberdeen "was a vile scoundrel who gave Apollo, one of the most daring rebel chiefs, information of the operations against the runaways, which he learned by listening to Mr Denbow's conversation." (CO 71/50)

1 NOVEMBER 1815

Almost one year had passed since Ainslie had left Dominica but he continued to marshall support, in this instance from WW Glanville, the former Attorney General and Judge Advocate in Dominica, who was also back in England. Lucas had blamed Glanville for the poor condition of the minutes of the trials, and at one time Ainslie had suspended Glanville for inefficiency.

Glanville's statement said:

> ... those Negroes in the island of Dominica who were tried by martial law that the parties had a fair trial and the proceedings were conducted according to military law. (CO 71/50)

21 DECEMBER 1815

Just before Christmas, however, Ainslie received news from Bathurst that he would not be returning to Dominica as governor but that his next posting would be as lieutenant-governor of the cold, small island of Cape Breton, off the coast of Canada. Bathurst's letter was more in sorrow than in anger. He acknowledged that Ainslie had acted with "zeal and good intention" but that there had been no need to maintain martial law and that Ainslie had acted with "so little discretion in the exercise of your authority as governor of Dominica that your return there could not be attended with any beneficial consequences".

It was a British response to a colonial problem: Ainslie had overstepped the mark and had abused the perfectly adequate tools of British justice to contain any slave rebellion.

> I have had under my consideration the documents which I thought it necessary to require from the island of Dominica for the purpose of investigating those parts of your conduct for the explanation of which his Majesty's Government originally thought it necessary to require your presence in this country. I have also attentively perused the various papers upon which you have rested your vindication.
>
> It is with great regret that I acquaint you that the result has been a conviction that it would not be expedient to authorise your return to that colony as governor. For, although I am disposed to admit that, during the latter period of your administration, there was great apprehension of danger to the colony from the increased force of the runaway Negroes in the interior, and that measures of greater vigour were necessary for their suppression, yet I can discover no necessity for that repeated recurrence to the exercise of martial law, and that supersession by courts martial of the established tribunals of the colony, which has distinguished that part of your administration.

As soon as the runaway Negroes became too powerful for the control of civil authority, and so long as they continued in arms to carry on depredations under regular leaders, the proclamation of martial law and the employment of the troops against them were Acts as much of duty as of necessity, and so far your conduct merits the approbation which it has received.

But when the object of putting down those insurgents had been attained, and the mass of offenders had been secured, the colony had a right to expect an immediate return to the regular administration of justice.

The penalties imposed by the Acts of the legislature of Dominica upon runaways were certainly not inadequate to the offences, however aggravated by other circumstances.

The civil courts appointed by those Acts for their trial were easily assembled - they had on former occasions evinced no indisposition to punish with severity where severity was expedient - nor was there on the present occasion any reason to doubt their inclination rigidly to enforce the law. The subjection therefore of the island to martial law, expressly, as it appears, for the purpose of trying such offenders by courts martial can admit of no sense. It was neither required for purposes of examples, nor was it calculated to raise the character of the government, because there was always just ground for apprehension that officers who had been actually engaged in warfare against the prisoners would not bring with them into court feelings the best fitted to make them impartial judges. And as the courts in question were composed entirely of officers belonging to the Dominica Rangers, there was still further reason to fear that to military feelings they might add colonial prejudices.

In adopting the decisions of courts thus constituted, it equally behoved you to have proceeded with extreme caution. But I cannot observe that any peculiar care was exercised by you in the examination of their proceedings, or that you evinced any great discretion in the selection of proper objects for punishment.

And although His Majesty's Government are disposed to acquit you in this as well as in the other instances in which your conduct has been arraigned, of any systematic violence or cruelty, and are willing to acknowledge your zeal and good intention, yet they are nevertheless compelled to admit that you have evinced so little discretion in the exercise of your authority as governor of Dominica that your return there could not be attended with any beneficial consequences.

I have therefore been under the necessity of submitting to his Royal Highness the Prince Regent the propriety of superseding you in that command.

But as his Royal Highness feels that the length and merits of your former services give you a claim to consideration, and that your supersession may give rise to a misconstruction of the real ground on which it has taken place, more specially on the part of your enemies, whose hostility towards you appears to have originated in most unworthy motives, His Royal Highness has been pleased at the same time to signify his gracious intention of conferring upon you the government of Cape Breton, and I have, in consequence, to signify to you the commands of his Royal Highness that you do proceed to that colony at the earliest opportunity, and take upon yourself the administration of the government. (CO 72/11)

22 DECEMBER 1815

The next day Ainslie replied.

I have the honour to acknowledge your Lordship's letter of yesterday announcing his RH [Royal Highness] the Prince Regent's command to supersede me in the government of Dominica.

As that letter contains the first notice of disapprobation of that part of my conduct, which regards the courts martial constituted for the trial of the runaways, the papers your Lordship had previously under consideration could not contain any vindication of my conduct, respecting these courts; it becomes necessary (and I trust your Lordship will pardon me, for so doing, on account of the serious and to me the

Wellingore Hall, Lincolnshire, where Ainslie sometimes stayed on his return to England. It was the ancestral home of his wife.

> ruinous consequences of this premature decision) to lay before your Lordship, my answer to this communication, it appearing, that the constituting of these courts and certain parts of my conduct [two illegible words] have influenced your Lordship to form an opinion of want of discretion in the exercise of my government... (CO 71/50)

Ainslie defended his actions one by one, especially regarding the holding of courts martial and those who sat in judgment during martial law. He again stated how difficult it was to find Justices of the Peace to sit in civil courts, such as the courts of special sessions. He ended by claiming that:

> I trust that the explanation I have now given, added to the unanimous voice of the whole people of Dominica, White, Coloured and Black for my return (with the exception of four or five individuals) as the Saviour of the Island will induce His Royal Highness [to reconsider his decision]. (CO 71/50)

Ainslie never did return to Dominica. Instead, one year later he took up his new job as lieutenant-governor of Cape Breton. Once again he made enemies, falling out with local officials and he left, without a pension, in 1820. Thus ended his diplomatic career. For the rest of his life he lived in Edinburgh where he concentrated on his interests in antiquarianism and coins and published his life's work, "Anglo-French Coinage", in 1830. He died there in 1839.

Below: celebrating independence day in Roseau.
Right: remembering Jacko: pouring libation on the well, Old Market, Roseau, 12 July 2014

After
Memory and memorials

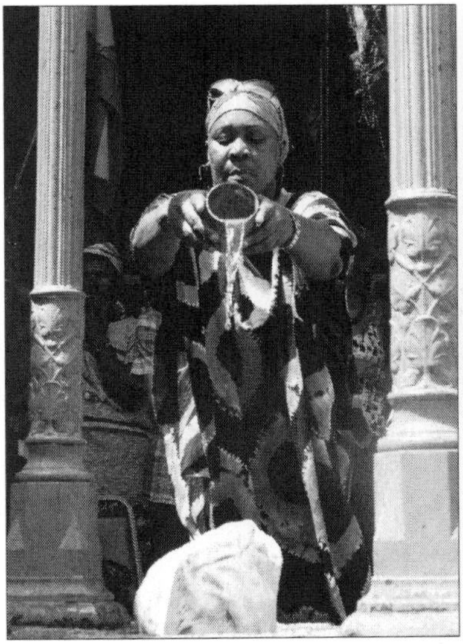

It is 200 years since the brutal onslaught of Governor Ainslie. The trials of 1813 and 1814, held in his name, mark the end of the Maroons as an organised force in Dominica.

But what is the legacy of the Maroons? The idea of an independently spirited people living off the land perhaps took root in those days of marronage. The post-emancipation communities in Dominica - with their ajoupas, provision grounds, use of traditional medicine, the inheritors of African folkways - may not have been very different from the Maroon camps of the interior. And today, while such communities have a modern countenance, old traditions and patterns of thinking remain, and the Rastafarian way of life in many ways echoes Maroon culture.

Dominica has been independent since 1978, yet until recently the Maroons have been absent from its official narrative. That changed in 2013 when the Neg Mawon Emancipation Monument was erected in Roseau. And on 12 July 2014, the life and death of Jacko was commemorated in Roseau's Old Market as libations were poured over the well, which had been tainted, as the Quaker Joseph Sturge wrote, by the blood of the executed. The spirit of the Maroons stirs again.

Maroon chiefs in profile

By the time of Governor Ainslie's arrival in Dominica in 1813, much of the interior of the island away from the coastal plantations was Maroon country: around Woodford Hill and Hampstead in the north; Rosalie and Point Mulatre in the east; River Claire, Giraudel and Morne Anglais in the south; the central forests of the upper stretches of the River Layou, and behind Colihaut and Dublanc on the flanks of Morne Diablotin in the west. Of the chiefs mentioned in "Your Time Is Done Now", we can locate Jacko, Noel, and Quashie in the Layou area, while Elephant was based in the south, and Apollo was possibly in the north.

From the documents used in this book, we can put together mini-profiles of the most important chiefs:

JACKO (sometimes spelt Jaco or Jacco), known as "the oldest chief" and the "supreme head" of the Maroons, lived in the forests on a ridge above the Layou River. He was a Maroon "for 46 years" according to Governor Ainslie. He was shot through the head at his Grand Camp in a surprise raid on 12 July 1814 by John LeVilloux, a Loyal Dominican Ranger, after Jacko had killed two Rangers, had wounded a third and was levelling his musket at another. Jacko's death was a turning point in Ainslie's war against the Maroons. African-born, and at one time "owned" by Beaubois of Castle Comfort, he is mentioned in the Maroon trials of 1786 as having led attacks on estates. At that time, he operated under the command of Chief Mabouya. His camp is mentioned by defendants during the 1813-1814 trials. For example, Joe said that he had been in Jacko's camp and had wanted to surrender following Governor Ainslie's proclamation, but believed that Jacko would kill him if he had caught him. Two women defendants, Adelaide and Rebecca, were captured in Jacko's camp in April 1814; it seems likely that the Rangers had penetrated his camp at that time but that it took them until July to confront Jacko. Today, Jacko is the one Maroon chief whose life has some physical legacy: the now named Jacko Steps, a set of steep and deep steps cut during his time into the cliff face, lead from the Layou River up to the "Grand Camp" on what is now called the "Jacko Flats", near the village of Bells. In reporting Jacko's death to Lord Bathurst, Ainslie said that Jacko had called himself the "governor of the woods".

QUASHIE (sometimes spelt Quashee, Quashy or Quasbey) is famous as having been the Maroon chief who, in May 1813, put a bounty of $2000 for the head of Governor Ainslie after the governor had offered $1000 for the chief's head. When Ainslie sent a messenger, a former Maroon, to Quashie's camp with news of the proclamation of clemency for those Maroons who surrendered, Quashie tried the messenger and shot him. According to evidence heard at the trials, when the Rangers attacked Quashie's camp in May 1814, they found 24 huts, four loaded muskets, gunpowder, clothing and "a considerable number of poultry". A Dominican Council report of 22 November 1814 said that Quashie and 27 of his followers had been rounded up in the middle of August 1814. An "old chief" of the same name, and owned by a man named Fagan, was banished in January 1815. (Chief Quashie should not be confused with Quashie from Woodford Hill estate who was executed for having given aid to the Maroons.)

ELEPHANT (also known as Policy) was killed in a Militia raid on his camp around present-day Giraudel, on the slopes of Morne Anglais, by Gabriel Beauchamp, the manager of Edenbro estate on 7 February 1814. Elephant, whose titular owner was George Anderson, is mentioned in the trials of Joseph, Victor and Joe, all of whom were charged with supplying the Maroons. In his memoirs Bremner said that before his own arrival on the island, Elephant had raided Anderson's cellar in Roseau and stolen Madeira wine and salted goods. In the trials, mention is made of Elephant visiting estates - once bringing his gun to be repaired. Both Victor and Joe were said to have been with Elephant when he was shot. In his affadavit, Alexander Labadie said that Elephant would have killed him had "he not been fortunately shot by Gabriel Beauchamp whose house he attacked in the open day accompanied by several of his followers with the determination of murdering them". Other planters said that Elephant's camp numbered up to 40 Maroons who were well-armed. Ainslie claimed, in a letter to Lord Bathurst, that Elephant had been hanged and his head exhibited in Roseau: this may be a reference to the practice of displaying the bodies of Maroons who had been killed elsewhere.

NOEL was based, like Jacko, in the upper areas of the Layou River. He was described by William Bremner as being among the "principal and most bloody" of chiefs, and was the last known chief to have been killed. On 9 December 1814, it was reported that Noel was surprised alone near his former camp in the heights of Layou by a party of Rangers. He was surrounded, and his "retreat into the thickets" was cut off. He refused to surrender, then he drew his cutlass and was shot by a Ranger called Joe Gibbon. The report stated that "he was found clothed in the uniform jacket of his unfortunate victim" - a reference to a Mr McFarlane, whom Noel had killed during an attack on his estate in the Layou Valley. Earlier that year, in April 1814, the Rangers had raided his camp, and according to minutes of the trials of Julien, Jane and Selimene, all charged as runaways, Noel had shot at the Rangers and was himself shot and wounded but he had survived that attack. Noel's head was taken to Roseau and exposed on a stick in Roseau.

APOLLO was a chief, possibly based in the north of the island. He featured in the court martial of Beauty, his former wife, who was accused of supplying the Maroons. According to witnesses, Beauty gave Apollo gunpowder, rum, sugar and salt and that, in return, Apollo brought her ground provisions such as yams and tannias. It was claimed in the trials that he was in communication with

Quashie of Woodford Hill who told him about planned attacks on the Maroons. Described by William Bremner as among the "principal and most bloody" of Maroon chiefs, and by Ainslie as one of the "most daring rebel chiefs", he was "still at large" in August 1814 and had escaped at the same time as Beauty had been taken. Apollo surrendered, according to Bremner, later that year having been pardoned by Ainslie; he became "a trusty guide" in the Rangers.

LOUIS MOCO was noted by Bremner, along with Apollo and Noel, to be a 'principal and most bloody chief'. However, on 19 March 1814, the Dominica Journal reported that "The private camp of the chief, Louis Mocho [sic], has been discovered and destroyed; a great quantity of baggage, poultry, stock, furniture etc etc carried away by volunteer Vidal, with a party of Rangers." According to Bremner, he was shot soon after Noel, in late 1814, by a Ranger called Joe Gibbon. His name, Moco, may refer to the Fula word moco'o meaning medicine man or to moko, a West African word for protector.

MOCO GEORGE (or George Moco), once owned by Mr Blondel, was killed by the Loyal Dominica Rangers on 20 April 1814. His camp was near Morne Trois Pitons in the centre of the island. His head was cut off and exhibited at Portsmouth.

GABRIEL was a chief, killed by the Loyal Dominica Rangers on 30 April 1814. His owner was listed as "unknown" suggesting he had been in the forests for many years.

In addition to the chiefs, there were those among the enslaved who supported the Maroons and were vital to their survival. Foremost among them were **PETER** (see pages 43-52), from the Hillsborough estate at the mouth of the Layou River, and **QUASHIE** (see pages 90-95), from Woodford Hill. Both were executed.

Endnotes

INTRODUCTION

1. A Collection of Plain and Authentic Documents in Justification of the Conduct of Governor Ainslie (London, 1815) p18
2 Ainslie to Bathurst, 21 March 1814, CO 71/49
3. ibid
4. Minutes of the Council of Dominica, House of Commons Parliamentary Papers Online, 10 July 1812
5 Stephan Timothy Lenik, Frontier Landscapes, Missions and Power: A French Jesuit Plantation and Church at Grand Bay 1747-1763, PhD dissertation, Syracuse University, 2010
6. Thomas Atwood, The History of the Island of Dominica (J. Johnson, 1791), p228
7. ibid
8. Jonathan Huddleston, And the Children's Teeth are Set on Edge (2011, www.tioli.co.uk), p260
9. Lennox Honychurch, Negre Mawon, The Fighting Maroons of Dominica (Island Heritage Initiatives, 2014)
10. CO 71/48
11. Unpublished memoirs of William Bremner, p 104 referring to year 1811.
12. See Parliamentary Debates from the Year 1893 to the Present Time, vol 31, from p596 for a full account of the events in Grenada
13. A Collection of Plain and Authentic Documents, p41
14. ibid, p6
15. LA Roberts, unpublished talk to Dominica Grammar School Historical Society, 9 May 1966
16. CO 71/49
17. RW Kostal, The Jurisprudence of Power, (Oxford University Press, 2008), p11
18. House of Commons debate, 2 June 1815, vol 31 cc596-606
19. See William Bremner's account of the Hillsborough uprising, page 44 and following pages
20. CO 71/51
21. Atwood, p241

1813 SUPPRESSION OF THE MAROONS BEGINS

1. Minutes of the Council of Dominica, House of Commons Parliamentary Papers Online, 10 July 1812
2. Bremner, p104
3. A Collection of Plain and Authentic Documents in Justification of the Conduct of Governor Ainslie (London, 1815), p39
4. The Examiner, April 3 1814
5. Ainslie to Bathurst, 21 March, 1814, CO71/49
6. Bremner, p142
7. In 1826, the UK Parliament published a report, the Second Report of Commissioners on Civil and Criminal Justice in the West Indies. In answer to whether slaves were provided with legal assistance, the investigators were told by an un-named legal figure in Dominica: "I have known counsel employed in these courts, and often their owners take an interest in their defence. Yes, I have known owners employ counsel for them, and I have sometimes

requested counsel to attend to them when I saw occasion, but there is no public defender."
8. Elsa Goveia, The West Indian Slave Laws of the 18th Century, chapters in Caribbean History 2 (Caribbean Universities Press, 1970)
9. Ainslie at one point suspended Glanville as attorney general because of his "repeated neglect of and inattention to the duties of his situation": letter from Ainslie to Bathurst, 16 February 1814 (CO 71/49). However, he remained in his post and continued to serve as Judge Advocate throughout the courts martial and courts of special sessions of 1813 and 1814
10. In this usage, "intercourse with" means to have dealings with or communication with
11. CO 71/48
12. CO 71/48
13. Michael Craton, in Testing the Chains, Resistance to Slavery in the British West Indies (Cornell University Press, 1982) argues that hurricanes were an important cause of the defeat of the Maroons (p232). William Bremner, in his memoir, suggests that the laying to waste of provision grounds and so on following a hurricane made the slaves more intransigent.
14. Minutes of House of Assembly, Dominica archives, Roseau
15. CO 71/50

1814 UP AGAINST MARTIAL LAW

1. Although the first court martial opened on 15 January 1814, Ainslie said he did not declare martial law until 16 January; Benjamin Lucas, senior member of the Council and Commander in Chief after Ainslie's departure, said martial law was declared on 12 January.
2. There is some confusion as to the name of the manager of the Hillsborough estate. A Mr Henderson was manager of the estate according to the minutes of the trials; William Bremner, however, named Mr Venn, also a witness at the trial of Peter and the six other defendants from Hillsborough, as the manager. It may be that Mr Venn was the overseer.
3. Joanneses, also called Joes, were Portuguese coins used as currency.
4. BW Higman, Slave Populations of the Caribbean, 1807-1834 (University of the West Indies, 1997), p200
5. While Rachel received 30 lashes as recorded in the lists of defendants, the trial evidence noted "lashes remitted".
6. A moco was a silver coin used in Dominica at the time.
7. Minutes of the House of Assembly, Roseau, Dominica, 1813-1815
8. *Content* is the French Kweyol word for a basket carried on the back.
9. A pass was a piece of paper giving a slave the right to leave an estate.
10. The runaway owned by Wallace is not listed in the official documents as having been killed.
11. Published in the Observer newspaper, London, on 22 May 1814.
12. In 1796, captured Maroon women were offered leniency in exchange for information. See Lennox Honychurch, Negre Mawon, p113

13. The last attack by the French on Dominica was in 1805.
14. Hester bore her child and died in jail on 24 March 1814. Her head was cut off, her body suspended for 24 hours and then burned.
15. Roger N. Buckley, The British Army in the West Indies, Society and the Military in the Revolutionary Age (University Press of Florida, 1998) p 226
16. Zabet was hanged; Rebecca was pardoned at the gallows.
17. George Moco may be the same person as Moco George, who was listed as having been killed on 20 April 1814.
18. The Scots Magazine and Edinburgh Literary Miscellany, Volume 76, Part 2, p546
19. The crapaud (Leptodactylus fallax) is an edible toad endemic to Dominica.
20. The word "case" possibly refers to the French Kweyol word for "house".
21. The correct name was Motard Belair.
22. Ainslie to Bathurst, 22 December 1815. Ainslie claimed that martial law continued until the end of March with the occasional sitting after that lasting for 24 hours. Certainly, four one-day courts martial were held through April and May, the last one being on 22 May.
23. Ainslie to Bathurst, 24 August 1815, CO 71/51
24. Minutes of the House of Assembly, Dominica, 1813-1815, p213
25 Thomas Southey, Chronological History of the West Indies, vol 3 (Longman, Rees, Orme, Brown, & Green, 1827) p559
26. Marie does not appear in the court records again.
27. Minutes of the House of Assembly, Dominica, 1813-1815, p233
28. ibid, p217
29. Hampshire Chronicle, 20 February 1815

1814 A GOVERNOR'S DEFENCE

1. Royal Cornwall Gazette, Falmouth Packet and Plymouth Journal, 8 January 1814
2. Liverpool Mercury, 15 April 1814
3. Ainslie's information may have been at fault or he may have deliberately inflated his achievements. The camps, as Ainslie claimed, may have been destroyed but the chiefs, Jacko and Noel, were still alive at this point while Elephant had been shot dead earlier that month by the manager of Edenboro estate rather than hanged as claimed by Ainslie.
4. Chasseral or Chasseron are both mountains in the Jura mountain range in Switzerland. The hand-writing is unclear.
5. Sylvanus Urban, The Gentleman's Magazine and Historical Chronicle. From January to June 1814, p504
6. Minutes of House of Assembly, Dominica, 17 April 1813 to 28 November 1815, p199
7. A Collection of Plain and Authentic Documents in Justification of the Conduct of Governor Ainslie (London, 1815) p18
8. Thomas Southey, Chronological History of the West Indies, Vol 111 (London, 1827) p556
9. ibid, p559
10. Scots Magazine and Edinburgh Literary Miscellany, Volume 76, 1814, p546
11. Southey, p559

1815 MAROONS DEFEATED, AINSLIE SACKED

1. Ainslie to Bathurst, undated, 1815, CO 71/50
2. Minutes of the House of Assembly, Dominica, 10 January 1815
3. Ainslie to Bathurst, CO71/50
4. Noel was identified as the murderer of Mr McFarlane.
5. Minutes of the House of Assembly, Dominica
6. ibid, 7 May 1815
7. Armatrading sat as President (judge) at some of the 1814 courts martial.
8. DR Fisher, The House of Commons, 1820-1832, vol V (Cambridge University Press, 2009)
9. House of Commons debate, 2 June 1815, vol 31, cc596-606
10. Sir Robert Heron, Notes (Grantham, London, 1815), p60
11. A Collection of Plain Authentic Documents in Justification of the Conduct of Governor Ainslie (Lowndes, London, 1815) p46
12. House of Commons debate, 2 June 1815, vol cc596-606
13. Memoirs of the Life of Sir Samuel Romilly Written by Himself, Vol 3 (John Murray, London, 1840), p177
14. Quashie is also spelled Quashee, Quashy and Quasbey.
15. Romilly, p179
16. CO 71/50
17. The Marshal or Provost Marshal was in charge of the jail.
18. These were the warrants for the execution of Caliste, Quashie and Charlie (CO 71/51)
19. This list is presented here in a different format from the original but uses the original language.

Bibliography

Anonymous, *Sketches and Recollections of the West Indies* (Smith, Elder & Co, 1828)

Atwood, Thomas, *The History of the Island of Dominica* (J. Johnson, London, 1791)

Buckley, Richard, *The British Army in the West Indies, Society and the Military in the Revolutionary Age* (University Press of Florida, 1998)

Bulmer-Thomas, Victor, *The Economic History of the Caribbean Since the Napoleonic Wars* (Cambridge University Press, 2012)

Collection of Plain and Authentic Documents in Justification of the Conduct of Governor Ainslie (London, 1815)

Craton, Michael, *Testing the Chains, Resistance to Slavery in the British West Indies* (Cornell University Press, 1982)

Dominica. An Account of Runaways Slaves, Killed, Taken and ... (ebook, Google)

Edwards, Bryan, *The History, Civil and Commercial, of the British Colonies in the West Indies*, vol 5 (T. Miller, 1819)

Epstein, James, *Scandal of Colonial Rule: Power and Subversion in the British Atlantic during the Age of Revolution* (Cambridge University Press, 2012)

Gott, Richard, *Britain's Empire: Resistance, Repression and Revolt* (Verso, 2011)

Goveia, Elsa, *Slave Society in the British Leeward Islands at the End of the 18th Century* (Yale University Press, 1965)

Goveia, Elsa, *The West Indian Slave Laws of the 18th Century, chapters in Caribbean History 2* (Caribbean Universities Press, 1970)

Heuman, Gad, *The Slavery Reader* (Routledge, 2003)

Higman, BW, *Slave Populations of the British Caribbean, 1807-1834* (Johns Hopkins University Press, 1984)

Hochschild, Adam, *Bury the Chains: The British Struggle to Abolish Slavery* (Pan Books, 2006)

Honychurch, Lennox, *The Dominica Story* (Dominica Institute, 1984)

Honychurch, Lennox, *Negre Mawon, The Fighting Maroons of Dominica* (Island Heritage Initiatives, 2014)

House of Commons, Parliamentary Papers (http://parlipapers.chadwyck.co.uk/marketing/index.jsp)

Huddleston, Thomas, *And the Children's Teeth were Set on Edge* (ebook, www.tioli.co.uk, 2011)

Journals of the House of Commons, vol 70, 1814-1815

Kostal, RW, *The Jurisprudence of Power* (Oxford University Press, 2008)

Laidlaw, Zoe, *Colonial Connections*, 1815-1845 (Manchester University Press, 2005)

Macaulay, Zachery, *Anti-Slavery Monthly Reporter*, vol 2 (London Society for the Mitigation and Abolition of Slavery in the British Dominions, 1829)

Marshall, Bernard, *Maronage in Slave Plantation Societies: A Case Study of Dominica, 1785-1815* (Caribbean Quarterly, volume 22, Nos 2 & 3, June-September 1976)

McLaren, John, *Dewigged, Bothered and Bewildered, British Colonial Judges on Trial, 1800-1900* (University of Toronto, 2011)

Mullin, Michael, *Africa in America, Slave Acculturation and Resistance in the American South and the British Caribbean 1736-1831* (University of Illinois Press, 1994)

National Archives, United Kingdom: *CO 71/48; CO 71/49; CO 71/50; CO 71/51; CO 72/10; CO 72/11*

Oliver, Vere Langford, *More Monumental Inscriptions: Tombstones of the British West Indies* (Borgo Press, 1993)
Price, Richard, *Maroon Societies: Rebel Slave Communities in the Americas* (Johns Hopkins University Press, 3rd edition, 1996)
Roberts, LA, *The Runaway Slaves (Negres Marons) of Dominica* (lecture notes, May 1966)
Romilly, Sir Samuel, *Memoirs of the Life of Sir Samuel Romilly* (John Murray, 1840)
Southey, Thomas, *A Chronological History of the West Indies*, vol 3 (Longman, Rees, Orme, Brown & Green, 1827)
Thompson, Neville, *Earl Bathurst and the British Empire* (Leo Cooper, 1999)
Trouillot, Michel-Rolph, *Peasants and Capital: Dominica in the World Economy* (Johns Hopkins University Press, 1988)

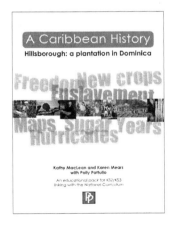

Index